Simon Connolly

THE NEW WINDMILL SERIES

General Editors: Anne and Ian Serraillier

196

THE DREAM-TIME

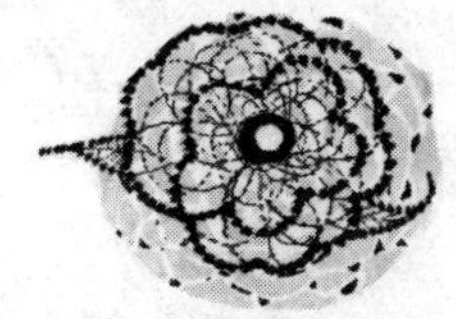

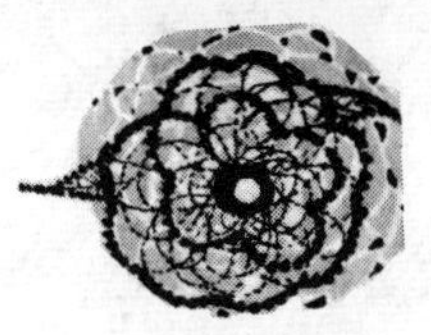

HENRY TREECE

THE DREAM-TIME

With a postcript by Rosemary Sutcliff

Illustrated by Charles Keeping

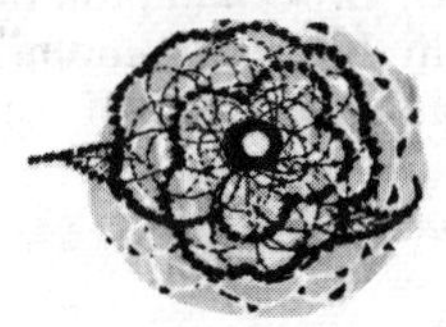

HEINEMANN EDUCATIONAL BOOKS
LONDON

Heinemann Educational Books Ltd
22 Bedford Square, London WC1B 3HH
LONDON EDINBURGH MELBOURNE AUCKLAND
HONG KONG SINGAPORE KUALA LUMPUR NEW DELHI
IBADAN NAIROBI JOHANNESBURG KINGSTON
EXETER (NH) PORT OF SPAIN

ISBN 0 435 12196 0

First published by Brockhampton Press Ltd 1967
First published in the New Windmill Series 1974
Reprinted 1977, 1979, 1983

Printed and bound in Great Britain by
William Clowes (Beccles) Limited, Beccles and London

The background figures used to indicate breaks in the text are taken from a drawing by Henry Treece and include, in his own words, 'the sun and the moon, the watching eye, the hunting man, the antler-pick, the leaves, the leaping salmon, the Old Man in his antlers, the spiked boar, the hand, the polished flints, the painted stones, the waves, the berries off the bushes—and lots of dark caves to go into!'

For RICHARD
and OLIVER KAMM
who are *the Boys*

Henry Treece

THE DREAM-TIME

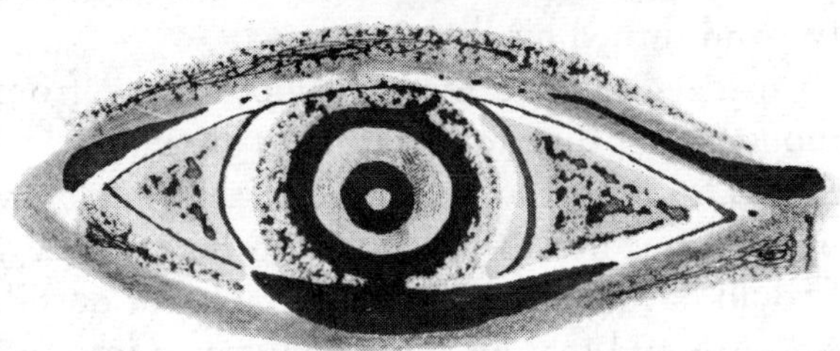

CROOKLEG lay in the darkest corner of the longhouse wishing he had not fallen out of the beech tree when he was gathering nuts and wishing that Holly the Old Man of the Dog Folk had known better magic for mending broken legs. Crookleg was afraid that his right leg would never be straight again to let him run with the other boys of the tribe. Besides, in its willow splints and with all the deerhide wrappings round it, it hurt, especially when the women rolled him over carelessly with their feet as they hurried up and down the long low room.

His mother Bluestone lay on a heap of brown fern at the far end of the dark room crying out and sometimes groaning. She had been doing this for three days and Crookleg wanted to crawl to her. But the priest woman with the black robe and the ash on her head always pointed her snake stick at him and told him harshly to stay where he was.

Her name was Ash and all the men were afraid of her—even Crookleg's father Thorn—and he was not afraid of much; not of the darkness and wolves and wild dogs. Only Holly the Chief was not afraid of Ash, because she was one of his women. But when she pointed at him he always crossed his fingers—even Holly—and turned his dark eyes away.

Ash had sent all the men and boys away from the longhouse when Bluestone started to groan. She would have sent Crookleg too, but some of the young women had begged her not to because with his crippled leg a wolf could have got him in the dark woods outside the village. Ash said that he could be lowered into the flint mine on ropes, but the women said that he would die there too because it was a cold time of the year. So he was allowed to stay while the magic happened to his mother, though Ash made him turn his face close to the mud wall so that he should not see anything.

She kneeled by him and said bitterly, 'At these times all the men go away. It is not for men to see. Because you have stayed bad luck may come on you and your mother and your father. It may come on the one who is not yet with us. We shall see, but if bad luck comes and the little barley crop does not sprout we shall know who to blame. The Old Man will not like you then. He will give you to Bone. Then you will know what there is to shout about. The pain in your leg will seem nothing.'

Crookleg shivered at this. Bone was the Rainmaker and lived in a little cave deep in the forest. The women took food to him and laid it outside the door. The men laid out flint knives they had made or small tender deer they had caught. Last year they laid a brown bearskin from a beast that they had lured into the pit with the sharp stakes at the bottom. Bone only came into the village through the oak stockade at the barley blessing time before the grain was put in the earth; and at the time of late-year fires when the stubble was burned and there was dancing to give thanks for the harvest. When he came, three boys went before him swinging bone bull-roarers to make the right terrible music for such a man.

Bone was very old and bent and no one had seen his face behind the leather mask that witch doctors always wore. This mask was shaped like a stag's head with the white antlers on the top of it. His eyes stared out of holes in the mask. His mouth gaped to show the flint teeth. Behind the mask Bone's hair hung down very white and greased with sheep fat. When anyone of the Dog Folk broke the law they were tied up and taken to Bone. He punished them and they did not come back to the tribe again. Their bones were put up in an old elm tree until they fell apart. The ground below the tree was littered with old bones. The leaves fell on them every year and covered them, but they were there. You could feel them if you felt down.

Even the wolves were afraid of Bone and ran away with their tails down when he turned towards them in his antlered mask and with the rattle-stick in his hand.

Without Bone there would be no barley out of the ground and without Ash the fire would not flare from the struck stones. Without Holly there would be no victory against the other tribes from beyond the forest—the Eagle Folk and the Fox Folk. Crookleg's father Thorn was the war-leader and could throw a spear into a striped lynx from twenty paces; but unless the Old Man Holly touched him on the forehead and right hand before the war-men went out, no luck went with them and they brought their warriors back on hide blankets to the village, groaning.

Crookleg wished it was not like that. He wished that things could be happy all the time and the sun shining, without having to go off with spears and bows to fight the other folk. He thought that if all the tribes would only sit round a big fire and talk about what made them angry with each other, then they need not throw spears and shoot arrows to make wounds. But this had never been done and he did not dare tell Holly, or even his own father, about it.

Then suddenly his mother began to howl out more than ever and he wished he could go to her. The women were sitting round her now, not even looking at her, and singing a very merry song that only the women of the Dog Folk knew. It was not in the men's language, so Crookleg did not know what it was about. That was another thing he would like to change. He wanted all the tribe to understand one another. But when he said this to his father once, Thorn glared at him so fiercely that he knew he had said something bad. Holly sent for him soon after this and said, 'Do you dream, boy?'

Crookleg nodded, looking at his feet. Then Holly said, 'If you say bad things again, Ash will be in your dreams. She will show you things in your dreams that will frighten you, and she might even speak to the King Wolf about you, and then he would wait in the wood for you. Do you want that to happen?'

Crookleg shook his head, so Holly sent him away and none of the other boys of his year spoke to him for a week.

Lying in the longhouse with his mother crying, Crookleg wished that a wolf bigger than any other wolf would leap over the tall stockade one dark night and eat up Ash, so that there was only her black robe left.

Then suddenly she was sitting by him and saying, 'You are not like the other boys. You cannot throw the spear very far. You have never even killed a wild cat. You cannot strike the fire from flint. What use are you in the tribe?'

Crookleg did not answer her because he knew that she would come into his dreams if he did, as the Old Man had threatened.

She said, 'Your mother is going away from the tribe. The little thing called Bud has already gone before her. It would be as well if you went too. We could do without you. You are useless to the folk.'

Then she got up and led the women in another song.

Crookleg did not understand what she had meant. He was very angry with Ash and wanted to hurt her. With a little twig in the soft earth by his fern bed, he made the shape of a big wolf. It had its jaws open and was leaping at someone. Crookleg knew what that wolf wanted to eat, but he did not dare say it even to himself.

Just then one of the women passed by him carrying a limp bundle. She stopped and cried out, then ran back to Ash and said, 'He is trying to hurt us all, he is trying to kill the tribe. Look what he is saying with that twig!'

Ash came to him again and looked down at the leaping wolf in the earth. Then she suddenly rubbed it out with her foot, fiercely. She said, 'Why do you hate us so? Why do you try to work the bad magic on us all? You are not good to have in the tribe. Something bad is in you and the Old Man must know. I shall go and tell him now.'

Then three of the women picked him up and flung him outside the longhouse into the bracken. They did not look at him when they did this in case the magic of his eyes would give them a disease.

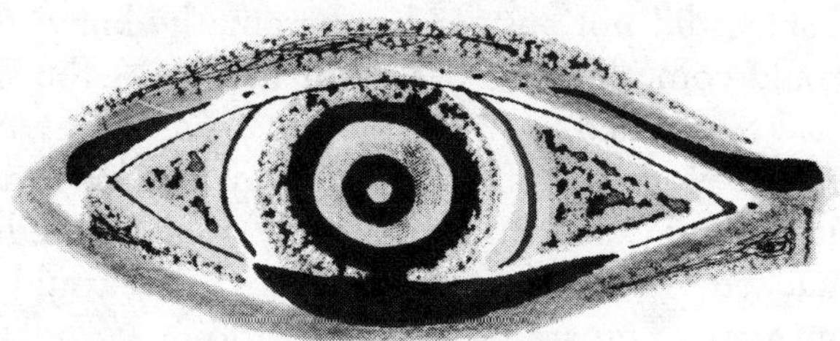

HIS FATHER Thorn came to him at dusktime and seemed almost afraid to speak to him. But at last he said, 'Holly is very angry. It has been three men's lifetimes since one of us made an animal in the earth, and ten since we made one on the rock walls. We have learned that it must not be done. Not even Bone may do it. The Dark Ones in the wood do not like it. It is forbidden to make shapes.'

Crookleg said, 'I was not making magic, Thorn. It came into my hand to do it, but I meant no magic. Where is Bluestone?'

Thorn stood away from him, thinking. Then he said, 'Bluestone was making the women's magic so that another should come into the tribe. Then suddenly she stopped crying out and did not move any more. The one she gave us did not move either. It was called Bud. They have both gone away. They will lie under the long hill on a bed with a hide over them and tall stones above them. If they wish to come back, they will. If they do not, they will not. There is no more to be said. It is as well they have gone away, since you are making magic, because your magic will stop the barley from springing and the deer from running into our pits. There will be no food for any of us if you keep doing this bad thing.'

Crookleg wept then. He thought that he had sent his mother and Bud away because of the wolf he had drawn in the earth. But Thorn poked at him with his spear-stick to quieten him, then said, 'Holly does not want to tell Bone about you. Bone might have you put up the tree. Holly wants all the young men he can get for the next fighting.'

Crookleg said, 'Why will there be fighting?'

His father said, 'If the barley does not spring this year, we must go to the Fox Folk and take their sheep. We must eat. They will not give us their sheep, so we must fight for them. That is the custom.'

Crookleg said, 'It is said that away over the big hill, four days of running, there are folk who take their food out of the sea. We could go to them and give them flint arrows for that food from the sea.'

Thorn was so angry he almost struck the boy with his spear-stick. He said, 'What are you saying? That food is unclean food. It would have scales grow on us if we ate it. They are bad folk by the sea. Their smell is not our smell. Do you want our tribe to disappear? Are you trying to kill us all, with your wicked ways?'

Crookleg shook his head and did not say any more. His father gave him a piece of dried meat cut in a strip, and a clay cup of water. Then he left him.

After that no one would speak to him or even look at him for a week. He wished he could be under the long hill with Bluestone and Bud, under the hide blanket sleeping. It was cold lying out there in the bracken, and hearing the wolves howling beyond the stockade every night, and scratching with their long claws.

THEN HIS leg got better. He could walk on it and almost run if he leaned on a stick. So he went to the men's longhouse and stood by the doorway until they grinned at him to come in. They were sitting in a ring talking and showing their big arm muscles. Crookleg thought how fierce they looked with their black hair pulled through round marrow-bones at the back and their faces and bodies all covered with the blue marks that Bone pricked on to them with a little sharp needle.

One of them wore a bracelet made from a ring of bull's horn. It made him look very important. His name was Fang and he was the one who would lead the war-folk when Thorn went away under the long hill at last.

Fang saw Crookleg and laughed at him then said, 'What magic are you doing today then, warrior? Are you fetching the bears to eat us all up this time?'

One of the men picked up a stone and threw it at Crookleg, but it missed. The man said, 'See, I never miss what I throw at. But he has a magic that turns the swift stone away. There is something bad about him.'

Then they all began to laugh at him and point and he knew happily that they were only making fun with him. Fang shouted out, 'Come nearer the fire, Crookleg. We have something good to say to you.'

He went bowing his head before his father because Thorn was the war-chief. Thorn caught him by the arm and drew him closer then said, 'See, I am giving you the blue stone that your mother wore round her neck. You shall wear it round yours and then all the other folk will know who you are. I had meant to give it to the new woman I would capture from the Fox Folk. But then I had a dream and in it Bluestone told me to give it to you. So put it about your neck. It is yours.'

Crookleg did as he was told. The stone seemed warm on his bare chest as though his mother's warm hand was touching him. This made him shiver a little and then cry because he had lost her.

His father said, 'You are a lucky boy, Crookleg. Today we are planning the fight against the Fox Folk.

We shall bring back sheep for the people and I shall get myself another woman for my house. So you are lucky to be with us here by the fire. You cannot run very well, but the men think that you could hold a spear-stick and stay at the back. It is time you saw fighting and began to learn what a man must do.'

Crookleg put on a hard face because he did not dare tell his father before all the men that he did not like fighting. Then Fang said, 'Show us, Crookleg, which finger you use when you draw the wolves in the earth.' He was speaking very slyly, looking like a wolf himself.

Crookleg said, 'I do not use my finger. I use a stick.'

His father said, 'But you use your hand to hold your stick. So show us which finger you use to guide the stick to make wolves.'

Crookleg held out his right forefinger and said, 'This is the one that guides the stick.'

Then Fang said, 'You know that when our boys become war-men they must make an offering?'

Crookleg thought that they wanted him to draw another wolf and he nodded his black head.

Fang laughed and said, 'Aye, you know well enough. And do you agree?'

Crookleg nodded again. He looked round the house to see where he might draw a wolf. It would need flat earth and a big space that no one would tread on to wipe out the picture.

Fang said, 'Then if you agree we shall take you to the fighting to get a taste of it and to see if you are brave and then when we come back we will make you a man of the tribe. And we will take the finger that guides the stick as your offering. Then you shall dip your hand in the wet clay and place it on the rock wall so that the shape will always be there and all the people will know what offering you made.'

Crookleg clenched his right hand and felt how good it was to have his forefinger. Without it he could not make pictures any more. He did not want to lose it just to be in the fighting.

But his father was looking so proud then, with the bunch of hawk feathers in his hair and the blue marks across his cheek-bones, that Crookleg did not dare draw back or weep or run out of the longhouse, though he badly wanted to.

Fang gazed at him a while then said, 'Yes, you will be a man yet. We thought you would scream or try to run away, and then I should have had to throw my spear at you. But you are braver than we thought. Now lie down in the corner on the sheepskins and sleep. We shall go off through the woods at dawn, before the Fox Folk are awake. That makes the fighting easier for us.'

But Crookleg did not sleep much. He kept trying to think what it would be like without his finger. He had always had his finger and now thought how much he liked it. He did not want them to knock it off with a stone axe. He even thought of getting up in the night and of running away somewhere, perhaps to the Fish Folk. But there was a guard by the door; and there was the high stockade to get over with the thick thorn bushes drawn across the gate space. And even if he got past the thorns there was the moorland to cross and there under the green-scummed pools were monsters with flint eyes and black scales on their bodies. All the men who travelled the moors at night had seen them.

So he did not run away but just lay on the skin and waited for the dawn when Fang would wake up the war-men and set them off.

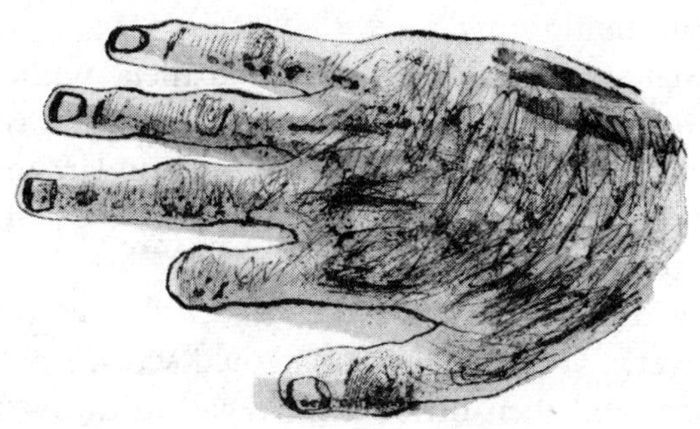

DAWN came too soon. And the Fox Folk lived too near. It seemed no time before the Dog Folk were climbing over the stockade and poking their spears through the wattle walls at the sleepers inside.

Crookleg had to stay on the far side of the stockade, holding a sharpened ash-stick. They would not let him have a flint spear till he had got back to the long-house and had given his offering in the presence of Holly and Bone and Ash.

He heard a lot of noise. Women were screaming. Then the Dog Folk were barking and the Fox Folk were howling. Then a big man in a black bearskin and a bone through his nose jumped over the stockade almost on top of him. Crookleg could see from the man's tattoo-markings that he was a Fox, so he pushed his spear-stick at him, but the man just brushed it aside with his hand and ran into the wood breathing hard.

Then some of the straw huts began to smoulder and send up black smoke and women tried to get over the stockade. Crookleg saw their fingers gripping the stakes. They were smaller than men's fingers. He did not stick his spear at them, because he thought of his mother Bluestone and did not like to do bad things to women. But none of the women got over the stockade. Their fingers loosened on the oak stakes and disappeared.

Crookleg felt sad. He did not feel like a war-man at all. Then suddenly Fang jumped over the stockade and shouted out, 'Run, Crookleg, run. Thorn has three arrows in him and is lying on the ground. He has gone away from the tribe. The men will not follow me yet, they want to go home. Run after me. I will lead you.'

Crookleg hobbled after him for a while, then was too tired to go on. His leg began to hurt too much. He fell sideways under a gorse bush and tried to get his breath. Many Dog men raced past him barking, but they did not smell him. He lay still until the last of them had gone by. Suddenly he thought: *Bluestone has gone away. Thorn has gone away. If I go back they will take my finger and make me into a war-man. Among the Fish Folk perhaps they do not take fingers. Perhaps they do not fight with stick spears. Perhaps they do not have barley sowings and men hanging from the elm tree. Perhaps.*

He waited a long time, till the sun rose up over his head and the flies came swarming out of the fern and buzzed over him, and the little grey snakes slithered past him into the heather.

No one came from the Fox Folk. He could smell their village burning when the wind shifted. He could not hear anyone shouting or laughing.

At last he got up and found that he could stand on his crooked leg quite well again. He forgot about his spear-stick and went on through the wood, sniffing for wolves, and trying to remember where he had been told the Fish Folk lived. He knew that at dawn in springtime they lived in a straight line from his own village, if you kept the low sun between your two eyes, in the middle of your forehead. But he did not know where they lived if it was later in the day or later in the year.

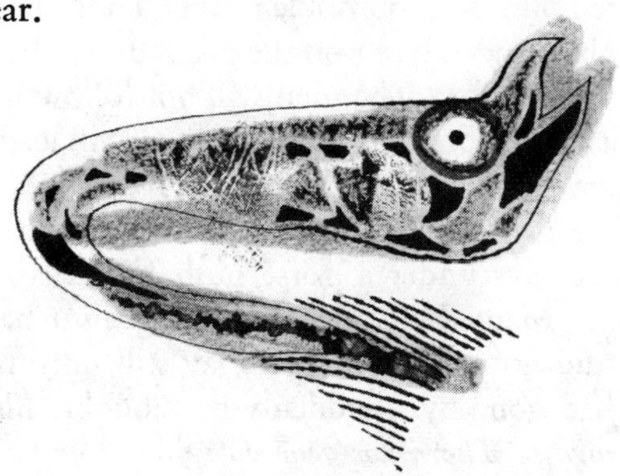

AT THE red time of the sun he came to a pleasant green place in the woods, where there was long green grass and a pool with little blue-green fishes in it. He put his hand towards them and they did not move from it. A hare came out of some foxgloves and sat near him, to look at him more closely. He said to the hare, 'Do you feed here, brother? Is there good food here?'

But the hare did not speak back to him. It kept on twitching its nose and turning its head from side to side to see him better. Crookleg laughed at the hare and said, 'I do believe that you are as silly as I am. They would never make a wolf of you, brother. Can you draw in the earth with your finger, then?'

The hare lost interest in Crookleg and slowly turned and shambled away, its white scut bobbing as it moved.

Crookleg drank some of the clear water and liked it much better than the water they got from the stream that ran into his village. No sheep had left their droppings in it. No folk had washed their hands and feet in it. He thought that a man could drink such sweet water with joy. At home you only drank when you were thirsty.

A brown owl fluttered down and stood on a branch only a spear's length from him and glared at him with amber-eyes. Crookleg said, 'Is this your pool, Old Man? Forgive me for taking water from it. I will draw the shape of you as payment. Then everyone will know it is your pool.'

He did this, in a stretch of flat damp mud that took the lines well, with a strip of spiked hawthorn.

It was so like the owl that Crookleg wanted to stay there always to be near the likeness. But the owl did not even look at it. He flew away, as low as a man's shoulder, staring into the grasses, flapping noiselessly.

Then Crookleg thought that his picture had not been so true, if the owl would not even look at it.

He still thought that it was good to keep his finger though. He was sad for Thorn to lie with three arrows in him, but that was always what happened to war-leaders and it was no great surprise. He was more sad about his mother, because she was warm and furry and gentle. She had never hit him. He was sad about Bud, because he had always wanted to hold a little man and to rub his cheek on the little man's and to listen to the funny words little men said before they started to say the words that war-men said. He liked best to hear their chuckling laughter.

Then he wondered if Bud was a little woman and not a little man. If she was, then she would speak some other language that he would never understand. That was not right, to speak and not to understand. He wished that all people, the men and women and hares and owls and dogs, could agree to speak the same words. Then all things would be so easy, to speak and to be understood. Perhaps no one would fight then.

He was turning this over in his head, like a pebble in the hand, when he almost jumped out of his skin, for someone was standing right behind him and sniffing at his back. He could feel the warmth of that sniffing.

He wished he had his spear-stick for a moment. Then he was glad he had left it behind. There was a girl behind him, not a war-man, and she was just like his mother, only his own age more or less. She had long reddish black hair down her brown back and a skirt of

yellow linen round her waist. On her thin arms she had two horn bracelets, and round her neck a hide thong with a piece of black stone on it, shaped like a tear that runs down the cheek. Her eyes were brown. In the ends of her ears there were the prettiest little red stones. On her russet cheeks she had the tattoos of a flower, it seemed, with petals and a round centre. On her body she had a pretty whirling shape like the thing a pool does when you throw a stone into it.

He said to her in Dog talk, 'Pull up your skirt to your knees and let me see your legs.'

There were enough words she knew, and she showed him how they had decorated her with the shapes of tree branches, with twigs and leaves and even apple-blossom.

She said in a funny, thick voice, 'Do you like that?'

He nodded. He said, 'They are apple leaves. The one who did that knew what to look for. He had eyes in his head.'

She said, 'My father did it. He was called Alder before he went away in the burning this morning.'

Crookleg said, 'Was he a Foxman?'

She nodded. 'There are none of my own family folk left now,' she said. 'I shall go to the Fish Folk. They do not raid villages. They spend their time taking the beasts from the sea. Perhaps they do not have magic either. I do not want any more magic. My father lost his finger for it and was never quite happy again. My mother lost her first baby. And see, I have lost the little toe on my left foot, because I did a dance that came into my head.'

Crookleg looked and said, 'A girl can spare that. It is not a great thing to lose. They wanted my best finger. This one.'

She didn't look. She said, 'My name is Blackbird. What do they call you—Crookleg?'

He nodded and said, 'Sit beside me. I am not a man so you need not sit behind me. We can be equals.'

She said, 'I had two hands of brothers from my father's women. They were all fierce Foxes, all had put the stick into a bear in the spring raging. All had lost something to the bears.'

Crookleg said in fear, 'What were they called?'

Blackbird said, 'They were all called Bear. One was called Bear Armless, another Bear Handless, another Bear Without an Ear.'

Crookleg said, 'I would not wish to offend them then.'

Blackbird laughed and went into the pool to wash her feet. She said, 'I think they were all in the burnt longhouse sleeping. Perhaps now they have their arms and hands again in the dream shape that comes after going away.'

Crookleg said, 'I still would not like to offend them. They would be even worse with their arms and hands to use spear-sticks with.'

She came out of the pool and sat by him. She laughed at him and said, 'They were not spear men. They were slingers. That is better than any spear man. I have seen them throw a stone through a hare and the hare went on running and didn't even know till later on.'

Crookleg said, 'I think I will go on my way through

the woods, Blackbird. I have far to go and do not want to waste the light.'

Blackbird got up too and said, 'Yes, let us not waste the good light. I am afraid of the wolves. I am a Fox, not a wolf. What are you?'

Crookleg did not like to say. But he did, in case Ash was listening and came into his dream again. He said, 'I am a Dog.'

Blackbird nodded and said, 'I knew you were. I saw you waiting outside the stockade with your spear-stick. I was only a few paces from you all the time you lay in the bushes. I thought I might put my knife into you at first, because of my father and my brothers; then when I saw you leave your spear-stick behind I thought I would come with you after all and not send you away into the silence.'

He said, 'I am glad you did not. I want to make pictures. See, there by the pool, I made an owl that sat on the low bough.'

She went over and kneeled above the owl. 'That is like my father's making,' she said. 'He would have welcomed you for his son. Did your father praise you?'

He said, 'No, my father was that war-leader with the three arrows in him. He praised only three arrow men. Men who could take three arrows in them before going away.'

Blackbird said, 'I do not understand men. They are so afraid of pictures, yet they will face a wolf or a bear.'

He said, 'I weep for Bluestone, my mother, but I do not understand women either. They are very fierce in their own way, and they speak words I do not understand. Do you speak the women's talk?'

Blackbird nodded shyly. Then she swept her red-black hair out of her eyes and said, 'The mothers start us at it before we learn the village words, the men words. We dream in it. Does that make you sad?'

Crookleg said, 'If we spoke the same words, we should be happy together. But we speak different words and that makes me sad.'

Blackbird went away to a holly tree and rubbed her back against it where she itched. Then she came to him again and said, 'I am going to do a bad thing. I will stop thinking the women's words. I will pray to the man stone. I will do all this because you can make pictures as old Alder did before the burning took him.'

Crookleg knew that she must be planning something and he said, 'No one asked you to, Blackbird.'

She put her fingers into his black hair and gave it quite a painful pull. 'Who needs to ask anyone anything,' she said, 'if only you do what you like to do?'

He said, 'Very well then, Blackbird. You tell me what we shall do.'

She said, 'We will go together to the Fish Folk. It will be safer with the two of us. The wolves are cowards and do not spring on two, only on one. Together we shall be safe.'

He said, 'That is true. We will go together and be safe.'

Blackbird said, 'And it will be warmer in this part of the year. We will share our warmth.'

He said, 'And that also is true. At my village I had

a deer hide to lie under. Now I have nothing to keep me warm.'

Blackbird got up from the grass and almost dragged him along. She said, 'You have something more than a deer hide, if you can make an owl that looks as though it could hoot and fly. That should keep you warm, to know that. It should keep your heart warm in you.'

He nodded and said, 'Yes, it has been with me all my time. It has kept me warm when the other boys got warm from fighting. But no one has ever said it to me before.'

She gave him a gentle push in the back. 'Well, I am saying it now,' she said. 'And my father Alder was a great chieftain. So I should know.'

ON THE way through the forest they came upon a dead ram. The black flies were round him and at first Blackbird wanted to go round them because the flies are a special folk with their own magic. But Crookleg said, 'Wait a while, his horns and hooves are still on. They could come in for something.'

So he went down into the hollow and took them.

For a while she walked a long way behind him waiting to see if the flies would follow. But then she came up with him and chattered on as merrily as before.

That night they slept in an oak tree, above the leaping-distance of wolves. And the next day they came to a place where grey clay lay above the chalk-stone. And Blackbird said to him, 'When a man makes friends with a woman he gives her something. What have you given me, but a lot of talk about your mother and Ash?'

He said, puzzled, 'What can I give you? I have nothing.'

She said, 'Do not look so frightened. I do not want your finger. But make a picture for me, make that owl again in this clay, and we will scoop it up like a stone for me to put on a thong.'

He did as she said, and the owl turned out well. It looked as though it could hoot and fly. She scooped it out of the clay with her long finger-nails and then dried it in the sun. It turned out to be a pretty shade of blue. But when she began to thread a hide thong through it, Crookleg said, 'It will go dry and crumble to dust. Can you make fire? I do not know how to.'

She laughed and said, 'Of course I can. All women can. They are the guardians of the hearth.'

He said, 'Then make one quickly and do not laugh at me so much. I will go and look round for a sleeping-place while you do it.'

When he came back she had a twig-fire blazing. He held sticks in this until they got black, then rubbed the black over the clay owl. And after that he held the ram's hooves over the fire until they melted, and with what melted he covered the black clay owl and then put it into the evening wind to dry.

'Now,' he said, 'you have something that will not crumble and will glisten. All folk will ask you of what stone it is made. You will be listened to with silence and no laughter. You will be great, wearing the black owl.'

Blackbird put on the owl and said, 'I liked it better when it was blue. And I do not want folk to be silent when I speak. I would feel wrong if that happened, because I am not great. I have no house, no fire, no baby of my own.'

Then Crookleg got angry and said, 'Why must you always think of these women's things? Why do you not think of me? Can I not make things that look as though they can roar or fly? Is that nothing? And do you ever stop to think that I have a lame leg? I have things to worry about.'

Blackbird ran away weeping, so fast that he could not catch her. But she came back to him when it was dark and they slept in a little hollow with a fire beside them that she made with the heather twigs he had gathered. So they woke up happily and found that the sun was shining again. Blackbird was pleased with her owl now

WHEN THEY reached the place of the Fish Folk at last it was not what they thought it would be. There were no houses and no stockades to keep the big sea out. The sea was much bigger than many packs of wolves and howled much louder.

The Fish Folk lived in little hollows in the cliffs

beside the sea. Crookleg did not like the smell of their shell-middens. They seemed a careless people. At home on the ridge all the leavings had to be burned or buried so that the dogs and wolves did not seek them out: but here the Fish Folk flung everything on the long shore, and never lit a fire to burn their rubbish.

He said, 'I do not think I shall stay here long.'

Blackbird wrinkled her nose. 'You are a flint-man,' she said. 'You are afraid of the blue water.'

He said, 'And so are you a flint-woman. What is the difference?'

Blackbird said, 'The difference is that I am a woman and you are a man. Women learn to live where their bread is. Men go looking for dreams, and die with three arrows in them, like your father. That is not wise.'

Crookleg said hotly, 'Then go and find your bread, woman. I give you leave to go. But I do not like the smell here, and I shall not stay.'

Blackbird said, 'If you think I shall give you back the clay owl you will make a big mistake. It lies so warm on me now that I could not part with it for a better man than you are, Crookleg.'

Crookleg shook his black head. 'I did not think of it,' he said. 'It has no value for me. I could make another. I could make a hand's count of others. Go, and take it with you, Blackbird, if you will not come with me to another place.'

Suddenly a man came up out of the cliff. He was two hands higher than Crookleg, and carried an axe made of whalebone, so broad and beastly that no man would have liked to face it. And this man also was broad and beastly, for his shoulders could not have got through the door at Crookleg's village. And his face was so savage that Crookleg thought there should be horns growing above his pale eyes.

And this man said, 'You, lame youth! Stop while I chop you down! What have you to offer? What treasure? What gifts? Do you know who I am?'

He came forward so grimly, his whalebone axe cradled in his arm, that Crookleg turned and began to hobble away. The Fish man shouted after him to come back and taste the edge of the whalebone axe. He was laughing when he said this. Crookleg glanced over his shoulder and saw that the man had half-forgotten him already and was now holding Blackbird by her hair and shaking her, still laughing as though she did not matter very much.

This made Crookleg very angry and he forgot to be afraid of the axe and went back again, looking for a stone he could throw at the man. The only stone he found was deeply embedded in the sandy shore that he could not pull out. So he grabbed up a handful of sand and white seashells and did his best to walk firmly forwards.

Blackbird called out to him, 'Go away. Go away. This man will hurt you, boy.'

While she was saying this she was also kicking at the man as hard as she could, but her bare feet did not hurt him. He screwed his hand round more deeply into her hair and shook her all the more.

Then Crookleg shouted, 'Stop that!'

The man did stop, and gazed at him. His pale blue eyes were hard to look at. Crookleg felt his own eyes going crossed as he stared at the man, because there seemed nothing to look at; it was as though there was no understanding behind the pale blue eyes, only a sort of emptiness.

Then the man said, 'I am Shark. No one tells me to stop anything I care to do. I am the Old Man here, and when I whistle all the fish come close to the shore so that we can eat them. I shall whistle to you now, and you will come close to me, and then I shall hit you with my whalebone axe. Is it agreed?'

Crookleg did not answer. He did his best to be very brave and to think of what he could do to hurt this Fish man. He flung the sand and shells at him, but the wind caught them and they flew away. Most of them came back over Crookleg's own arm and half-blinded him. And while he was spluttering, he heard the man whistling, and sure enough he felt his legs being drawn towards that red-haired brutish man.

And when he was within three paces of the man, the whistling stopped, and Shark said grimly, 'Now stand still, little one, and I will gaff you like a fish.'

Blackbird cried out, 'Run away, Crookleg. Run away. You are too weak to help me. What can you do against this chieftain?' Crookleg said, 'See if you can hold his arms and I will try to take his axe away.'

Shark laughed and swung Blackbird about as though she were just a dead fish herself. But at last she grasped his right arm and then Crookleg hobbled in and took hold of the axe shaft.

He had never held on to anything so fierce in his life. He saw Blackbird go flying away into the sand, and roll over and over. Then he felt himself being lifted and swung round, and in the end he had to loose the axe and go flying himself. He fell with his face in a shallow sea-pool with little shellfish in it. The water was very thick and strong and salty.

He drew his lips away from it and as he did this, the whalebone axe thudded into the little pool, just where his head had been. So he rolled over, and the axe just missed him again.

As he took his breath, to roll sideways once more, he heard the thudding of Blackbird's feet on the hard sand, and glanced up to see her fling handfuls of sand into Shark's face.

The man staggered back, rubbing at his eyes, his axe forgotten for the moment.

'Run, Crookleg,' Blackbird shouted. 'Get away from the shore while I keep him here. I will follow you. I will follow you. Run!'

So Crookleg got up and ran as well as he could, away from that dreadful place. But when he got up to the dunes where the coarse brown grasses were, he saw that Shark had caught Blackbird again and was carrying her off towards the caves in the cliffside.

He did not know what to do then. He felt more useless than ever before. He wished that he could use an axe and make folk like Shark afraid of him. He wept and hit his right hand against a rock, and wished he could not make pictures, and that he could fight instead.

Then at last the night came down and he made his

way inland and slept on top of a pinnacle of rock where nothing could reach him in the darkness.

THE NEXT morning he woke thinking of Blackbird, but he did not dare go back to the shore and see where she was. He had dreamt all night about Shark's red hair and pale eyes and his terrible axe. Now he felt sick even to think of him again.

So Crookleg climbed down from the rock pinnacle and went with the sun at his back so that he would get a warning of any shadow that came up behind him. He found a damp stone where there were snails crawling and ate some of them. The shells were very gritty in his mouth, but now he was getting too hungry to bother about that.

He chewed the leaves of a tree, but only to get the moisture from them. He did not swallow the pulp that was left in his mouth when the juice had gone.

He began to wonder if he dared go back to his own village, and tried to think which way he should go to get there. In the far distance, on a long chalk ridge, he could see three stones standing upright to mark the way somewhere—but he felt sure that this was not his country. He did not want to meet the folk of any tribe he did not know now. And even if he could find the way back to the Dog village, Holly and Ash and Bone the Rainmaker would be there, waiting to ask him where he had been, and why he had not reported back after the fight with the Fox Folk. Fang would be the war-chief there now, and Fang did not like him very much. He would ask for his finger again, and Crookleg could not bear to think of that.

He was so miserable, he began to weep and the tears ran down his cheeks as he ran onwards inland. A brown wolf with grizzled sides was standing under some overhanging oak boughs watching him with yellow eyes. But Crookleg didn't care at all. He ran quite close to the wolf, crying, and the wolf just stood and watched him without rushing out at him and pouncing. The wolf had never heard men making these sounds before and he thought that there must be some trick in it, to catch him. So he let the boy go on.

And by sunset Crookleg stumbled to a place where there was a curling blue river, and men sitting on it in skin-boats, fishing with lines. Smoke came up from the clustered huts among the reeds, and he could smell porridge being cooked. He was so hungry that he ran down into the village.

Close by the river there was a long shed without walls, its thatched roof supported on tree trunks with the bark still on them. Men and women and children were sitting under this shelter, and a young woman in a red linen cloak was ladling out meal-gruel into their bowls.

She looked up when Crookleg came round the side of the shelter and said, 'Who are you, then? If you want to eat with us you should have a porridge-bowl. We do not eat out of our hands like some savage folk inland. We are decent folk here.'

She went on with her work then and seemed to forget him. Some of the other folk looked back at him, not angrily but as though they had not seen anything like him before. A little girl came to him and put a wooden bowl into his hands and then went back to her mother.

So Crookleg took the bowl to the woman in the red cloak and she filled it without saying a word.

An old man with white hair touched him on the leg and showed him where to sit on the ground, and after a while, when his bowl was empty, Crookleg rose and gave it back to the little girl. He said to her, 'I am of the Dog Folk and they call me Crookleg.' But the little girl's mother said, 'I did not hear anyone ask where you came from or who you were. In this place we look after our own tasks and do not meddle with other folk. If you have something to tell, then go to the Headwoman who has fed you and tell her. That is the custom here.'

So Crookleg hobbled over to where the woman in the red cloak sat on her high chair and kneeling before her said, 'I am Crookleg from the Dog Folk. Thank you for the porridge, I was very hungry.'

The headwoman gazed at him then laughed and

shook her corn-coloured hair. 'You are lucky to be alive,' she said. 'There are no Dog Folk now. They burned up the Fox Folk and now the Badger Folk have burned them up, too. One of our folk sat in a tall tree yesterday and watched it happen. You have no house to go back to. You can stay here if you wish.'

Crookleg said, 'Who are you? If I stay with you, what will you make me do? What do you call the god here?'

All the folk in the long shelter were listening to him and whispering, then sometimes laughing at the strange way he said his words. The woman in the red cloak smiled down on him very kindly and held up her hand for all the folk to be quiet a while.

She said, 'We are River Folk—not sea-folk or forest-folk or hill-folk. We do not care where the river comes from, or where it goes to. It keeps passing by our village, and that is all we care about. And our lives are ruled by our river, who is the god that we pray to and dream of. If you wish to stay with us, you must learn to let all things pass by as the river passes. So, no more words from you. We will call you Twilight—because you have the hair of night time.'

She looked at him a while, then put out her hand and felt his hair with her long, white fingers. 'Yes,' she said, 'this is inland hair, twilight hair. So you know your name now. I am the lady here and no one questions my law. Do you question my law?'

Twilight said, 'I question nothing, lady. I am glad to have a roof over my head and a fire to sit by. I am not a war-man.'

She said softly, 'War-man? War-man? We set little store by war-men here. We live quietly beside the stream. It is only the inland folk who hurt one another. If you talk of hurting folk here, my people will send you away, or the fish-stick will go in you.'

He went with her then, down by the shallow stream, and saw the sheds where the women teased the wool, then put it on spindles and wove it into cloth. He saw the wooden vats where they dyed it in all the colours of the seasons—green for spring, yellow for summer, red for autumn and white for winter.

She said, 'Come now, Twilight, and we will see what the men do.'

He said, 'Lady, I am not a proper man. I am crippled in one leg—and I am not very brave either.'

She looked at him a long time, smiling out of her yellow-fringed eyes, then said, 'I can see that you have hurt one leg, slightly, and that you are gentle in your speech. But that is not how you describe yourself. No, Twilight, if you are fit to walk at all, you should walk with me.'

SO HE went with her to the men's place and saw the hides being stretched and limed to make them soft, and the fresh fish being gutted and prepared for the hearth fire.

And in one place Twilight watched men over the great oak buckets sniffing at the barley beer as it fermented.

He said to the lady, 'There are many things happening

in the world these days, lady. One would not think that so much could go on at the same time.'

She laughed and said, 'I am hardly older than you are, but I know that life does not stay still.'

She walked about the hall for a while, then she said, 'Some of my men have found a strange stone in their digging for flint. It is like no other stone. It bends and shapes to the hammer.'

She went to her coffer and came back with a piece of this strange stone. Twilight scratched it with his thumb-nail and found the marks shining brightly where his nail had been.

He said, 'I could scratch a wolf or an owl on this. I know their shapes by heart.'

She said, 'Better an owl than a wolf. I do not take well to those beasts. But do as you please. I shall like to see what you can make. Perhaps you could be useful in this village.'

FOR MANY days Twilight worked at the red metal. At first he thought only of owls, or of men with three arrows in them, or of women howling when they knew that Bud would not come to leaf.

Then at last he saw sense, saw that a beast with four feet, or with antlers, made a more pleasing shape to the eyes and to the fingers. And so he chiselled out a shape. A shape that could be looked at, or worn round the neck on a thong. Or, if it was big enough, even made into a shield for a war-man.

When Twilight had finished the copper brooch he gave it to the woman. She said, 'This is the most beautiful thing I have ever seen. Now I shall hide it away or news of it will get round and the Fish Folk might come to take it from me.'

Twilight said, 'I did not make it to be hidden away. It is to be worn round the neck on a thong for all men to see. What joy is there in making if no one sees the leaping beast?'

The woman smiled at him and said, 'Very well, I will wear it. But I shall always know that men are looking at it and wondering how they can get it for their own women.'

Twilight said, 'I have never wanted to fight before, but I would fight to protect that brooch. When a man makes a thing from nothing, with his hands, he loves it in a strange way, even though he gives it to someone. He always remembers it and keeps it warm in his heart. What is your name? I have not dared ask you before. I only dare ask you now because you like the brooch I have made for you.'

The woman with the golden hair said, 'My name is Wander. I shall always walk with three men at my back from now on. This brooch must be guarded. And since you have made it for me I shall let you walk with me, by my side, before the warriors. If you wish, I will tell the folk that you are my chosen one. Would you like to be a chieftain among my folk?'

Twilight shook his head. 'No, Wander,' he said. 'I am only a lame boy who likes making the shapes of beasts. If you made me a chieftain the folk would want

me to do other things. I am not very brave. I cannot use a spear very well. I do not know how to give advice to the war-men, or how to sow the grain at the right time.'

Wander laughed. 'Everyone has to learn, Twilight,' she said. 'Besides, the folk would be happy to have one among them who can make such brooches. They would not expect the other things from you. Turn it over in your head while you are working, and later I will ask you again.'

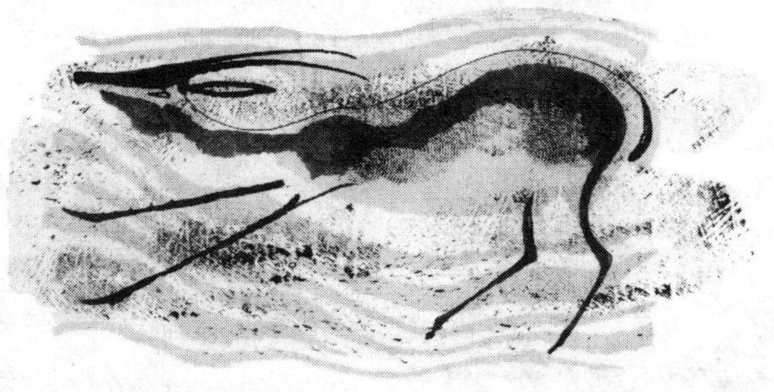

TWILIGHT stayed with them for many months. The folk brought pieces of soft stone and copper to him and asked him to make brooches out of them. They gave him a hut to work in, down by the blue river and left offerings of food and drink and deer hides in return for the things he made.

His head was full of shapes and his hands were hardly ever still. With his knives and chisels of bone and flint, he made the shapes of stags running, eagles flying, fish swimming and men prancing into battle with their spears in their hands and their wicker shields held before them. The warriors would come and lean at his doorpost every day, watching his swift hands at their work. One of them called Adder said, 'If I could do that I would be the happiest of men. Better to make such things than to stand alone against bears and wolves. If I had a son I would hope that he could do what you do. Could you show another man how to make such things?'

Twilight shook his head. 'I do not know myself how they will turn out,' he said, 'until I have made them. It is in my head and my eyes and my hands. It is not a thing that can be told to others.'

The warriors nodded and one of them said, 'It is as I thought, it is your own magic, only for you. If you passed it on to someone else, you would lose part of it and then your things would not be so good to look at.'

For the warriors Twilight carved knife handles and made the shapes of twining snakes round their spear shafts. For Wander he made another brooch, of a black stone that a boy found by the river. It was in the shape of a man's hand holding a wheat ear. When he gave it to her she said, 'Now you can never leave us, Twilight. Now I know what you are. You are a man who can fetch the corn out of the earth so that the reapers can hold it in their hands and cut it with their sickles. It is all clear to me now that if you left us our crops would stop growing and then we should starve. I ask you once more, will you be our chief and rule the folk, sitting beside me in the council hut?'

So Twilight gave in and did as she asked. The

River Folk sang and danced at this, and all in the village went about laughing at the thought that now they would never have a bad harvest again.

That year the barley came up out of the earth so thickly that a man could not put a finger between the shoots. It was the best crop the folk had ever known.

When Twilight passed along the path between the thatched houses, women came out and kneeled on the ground. Some of them asked him to touch their children when they had coughs or had broken a bone. They said that Twilight could make them well again. He did as they asked, but always told the women that his only magic was in his carving and drawing. They did not believe him, and thought that he was joking with them.

Then, when all was going well, one bright morning the boy who watched on the hill above the river came running into the village shouting that the Fish Folk were coming in their skin boats. Wander took Twilight on to the hill and pointed. 'He is right,' she said. 'I have never seen so many of them. There are two hands of them and three men in each boat. It is a war band and the chief in the first boat is called Shark. He has red hair and blue eyes and carries an axe of whalebone. He is the fiercest of men. It will not be easy for our war-men to drive them away. What shall we do, Twilight?'

He bit at his knuckles thinking. Then he said, 'Who am I to tell war-men what to do, I cannot fight?'

But just then Adder came running up to them and kneeled before Twilight. 'What shall we do, master?'

he said. 'There are two of them to one of us. What shall we do? You must tell us.'

Twilight said, 'If you fight they will kill us all and take the women and children away with them. If we run away they will take the village and the River Folk will never have a place to be in again. If I had to decide, I would say that we should talk to them and ask them to go back to their own place and leave us alone.'

Adder laughed behind his hand at this, but Wander nodded and said, 'If you say this, then we will do this. But they will not listen to us.'

In the village the River Folk were gathered, the women and children surrounded by a ring of war-men who were waiting with their spears stuck out.

Then the round hide-covered boats of the Fish Folk pulled in among the reeds and their war-men leaped out with their bone axes and came running. Shark led them, with white clay over his face and his hair greased and bound up on top of his head to make him look taller.

When Twilight saw him, he was very frightened. But he stood beside Wander and tried not to shiver. His face and hands were very wet as Shark came striding towards them, grinning like a sea monster, his blue eyes as sightless as flints.

So they faced one another, with only five paces between them, and were silent for a time. Then Wander said very bravely, 'What have you come for? Are there no more fish in the sea?'

Shark grinned worse than ever and said, 'There are

always fish in our sea. We do not go hungry like other folk. We are a lucky folk and a brave folk. Have you not heard?'

Wander said in her firm voice, 'I have heard many things of you and not many of them are good. What have you come for?'

Shark laughed back at his clustered war-men then said, 'We have heard of the pretty things you have here. We have heard of the one who makes them and who brings luck on your village. So we have come for the pretty things and also for the man. We shall take the things and the man back with us and shall hurt no one. If you will not give them up, we shall take them just the same, but we shall do other things as well, and you will not like what we do to you and to your village.'

Then Twilight felt all the River Folk looking at him, so he spoke up at last and said, 'If you take the things away, their luck will leave them and you will bring sadness on your village. And if you take me away I shall not be able to work for you. I shall not be happy with you and so I shall forget my magic. It will be a bad bargain for all of us.'

Shark said, 'You are braver now than when we met before.' He pretended to throw his axe at Twilight, but Twilight stood his ground before all the folk and did not move. Shark looked angry at this. No one outfaced him usually. He said roughly, 'When I speak, all the folk listen. I do not like it when a crippled fellow from inland stands against me with words. I shall take the things and you also. We will test your words then. If the things bring us bad luck, we will throw them into the sea, and the bad luck will end. And if you will not work for us, then we will see that you work for no one at all, for we shall hold your hands in the fire until they are burned sticks. What have you to say to that, lame one?'

Now all the River Folk gazed at Twilight and he suddenly forgot his fear. He turned to Adder and said, 'Lend me your spear, brother. The talk is ended. Who can expect a sea monster to understand the wisdom of men?'

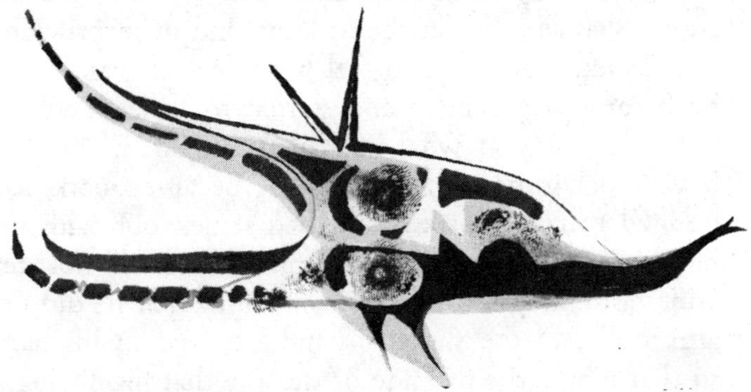

AT FIRST there was a heavy silence, then suddenly Shark began to laugh and all his war-men joined him, bending and slapping their thighs. Even the River Folk laughed a little, but most of them did it behind their hands.

Adder said, 'I will go in your place, Twilight. I might last a little longer against this man.'

But Twilight put on a hard face and said, 'Did you not hear me? Give me your spear. Why should you die for me? I did not ask you to.'

Adder gave him the spear and Twilight glanced round to see where there was space for him to move back when Shark rushed at him with that terrible axe.

He set himself, with one leg well behind the other, to keep his balance, then he said, 'Let us begin, if we are going to.'

Shark was still laughing and the water was running out of his pale eyes on to his brown cheeks. He stopped laughing suddenly and ran at Twilight without any warning. But Twilight had the luck to get his spear up and pointed at Shark's chest, and this stopped the rush. Shark looked at the little wound in surprise and put his left hand to it to feel how deep it was. Then he became very angry and started to yell. Twilight felt quite sorry at what he had done, but he did not have much time to feel like that because Shark had dodged round the spear and had struck out with the bone axe. Twilight saw it coming but could not step aside fast enough. Shark was so angry that he did not aim well and the slippery handle turned in his hand so that it was the flat side of the axe that hit Twilight in the ribs and not the keen edge. It knocked the breath out of him, but did not cut him. Now he was so furious that he forgot all fear and all sorrow, and before Shark could strike again, he poked the spear point at Shark's legs. Shark shouted out and began to hop round, saying what he would do in a moment. He even put his axe under his left arm so that he could bend and look at the cut in his knee. And as he did this, Adder whispered, 'Now, Twilight, now you can have him.'

Then Twilight poked out again and this time missed Shark, but knocked the axe on to the ground.

'Now, now, now!' the River Folk yelled.

But Twilight felt all the anger go out of him and he could not do it. He was suddenly shocked when Wander stepped forward and swept her foot out, knocking Shark off balance. And then Adder snatched back the spear and pushed it through the Fish chieftain into the ground.

Everyone began to scream out then, and the River Folk swarmed all over the enemy. Even the women and children hung on to arms and legs while the war-men used their spears and axes.

And when it was over, Fish Folk lay sprawled from the village gate across the barley field and right to the river reeds where their boats still waited.

Adder said laughing, 'They will not need their boats again. We shall use them. You did well today, Twilight. Now we have a war-chief among us. You did not tell us that you could fight as well as make brooches.'

Wander said, 'Go away, Adder, and see that all the Fish men are thrown into the river. It will carry them away from us. I do not want to see any more of them.'

Twilight said, 'I am so sick at what I have done I shall never take up a spear again. What I have done will stop me from making pretty things again. I did not know that I was such a bad man.'

Wander said, 'You are not a bad man. It had to be done and you were the only man who would dare do it. It is not a bad man who saves our folk as you have done. Now I have seen what sort of man you are, I am willing to kneel before you in front of the folk and call you my master. Then this tribe will be yours, and if you will take my hand, I will be your slave. I will cook your food and sew the hides to make clothes for you. You shall live in my house and call it your own.'

Twilight shook his head and said, 'You are the woman here. I am a stranger and no more. My teeth are chattering and my legs are shaking. How can you call me your master? I do not like myself now. I feel too sick to eat. I am worth nothing now.'

But Adder came back from the river and said, 'You are worth everything to us. No one has a chieftain like you. We shall take the boats and go down the river to the place of the Fish Folk. There will only be the old men and the women there now that we have put their warriors into the water. So we shall wipe them out and then our folk will never have anyone to fear again. You have brought this happiness to us, and you shall lead us in the boats to destroy them for ever.'

THEY SET off before the dusk came down. Wander went in the same boat as Twilight. Adder led the rest of the war-men. Wander would not let Twilight paddle the boat, but did it herself in homage to him. He tried to say that he would not go, but they would not listen to him. And that night they pulled in to the river bank close to where it met the sea. The next morning, before dawn, they rose silently and went on their way down the coast. Before the sun had got to its full strength they came in to the little haven where the village of the Fish Folk was. The Fish Folk thought that their own men were coming back, and ran down the shore to meet them.

Then they saw who it was and started to cry out and throw sand on to their heads. Some of the old men and women rolled on the shore in misery and stuffed shells and seaweed into their mouths. They were most afraid.

Adder called out for Twilight to let the war-men rush up and spear them as they lay, but Twilight said, 'No, they are suffering enough in their sadness. I am not the one to make them suffer more. Would you want your own old folk and women hurt?'

Wander said in a hard voice, 'You would wipe out a pack of wolves, wouldn't you? Would the Fish men have shown us any kindness? You will gain no love from these people by sparing them. They will not think you are a greater chieftain.'

Twilight said, 'I do not care what they think. I do not want anyone to love me because I spare their lives.'

Just then a group of the young women came down

the shore with ash on their heads, wailing, and Twilight saw that the one who led them was Blackbird. She did not know him for a time, and when she did she stood before him with her head bowed, waiting for him to have her speared.

He went closer to her and said, 'There is no cause to be afraid of me, Blackbird. Once you took care of me and led me through the forest safely. I could not hurt you after that.'

He smiled at her, but she did not smile back. She said, 'I left you on the shore here and went with Shark. You should punish me for that. I deserve it, so punish me.'

But Twilight took her by the hand and said, 'I do not think of it. Shark forced you to go. All has turned out well, so why should you think of it? Tell me, where is the clay owl I made for you when we were wandering together?'

Blackbird said, 'Shark would not let me wear it. He said it was too strong in magic for a girl like me. He put it on the shelf in his house to be prayed to and to bring luck to his folk.'

Wander said in scorn, 'It has not brought much luck. You might have been better off without it.' She did not like Blackbird.

Then she turned to Twilight and said, 'Who is to kill her, you or me? Some offering must be made for our good luck, or we shall have no more of it and our folk will not love you any longer. If you will not do it, give me the spear and I will do it.'

Then Twilight got very angry and said, 'How many

times must I tell you that there is to be no killing? If you speak of it again I shall walk over the hill and leave your tribe for ever. Killing must stop between tribes.'

When he said this, Wander looked at him very strangely. Then she turned and glanced at Adder and they seemed to nod to each other. But neither of them spoke and Twilight took no more notice of them. Instead, he told the women and old folk that they would be safe and need not wail and roll about on the shore any longer.

A few of the youngest war-men of the River Folk grumbled at this and made fierce faces, but Adder went among them and quietened them down. They whispered together for a while, then began to search the houses to see what they could find.

Not even Twilight could stop them from doing this, for it was the oldest custom and could not be broken.

But he saw to it that Blackbird got her owl back. Though when Wander saw it hanging round the girl's neck she said, 'Why did you never make one of those for me? I like this more than anything you have made for me. Tell the girl she must give it to me. I want it and I am the Woman of the tribe.'

Twilight said, 'I will make one for you, but the girl has a right to this one. It was made for her, and only for her.'

Wander frowned and said, 'This girl has no rights at all. She is my slave now, and I shall see that she does what I say, or she will suffer. All the bravery seems to have gone out of you, Twilight. You are not the man I thought you were.'

Suddenly Wander stepped forward and grasped at the clay owl on the thong. Blackbird cried out and tried to stop her, but she was not quick enough or strong enough. Then Wander found that the soft clay had broken in her hand. She flung it into the sea in anger and said, 'That was your fault, girl. You shall be whipped for not giving it to me when I asked for it.'

Blackbird began to weep then. Twilight said, 'Wander, the fault was yours, not Blackbird's. It is foolish for two women to quarrel over a little clay owl. Look, tomorrow I will go inland and find where there is clay. And I will make one for each of you. Then there will be no more tears and anger.'

Wander said, 'Then you must see that the one you make for me is prettier than hers. A slave must not wear a prettier thing than her mistress.'

By then Twilight was so weary that he said no more, but went to the men's longhouse under the cliff and lay down to sleep on a bracken bed.

THE NEXT morning he set off inland and followed a small brook. At last it led him to a shallow pool where there was clay. So he sat down in the sunshine and made two owls. He saw to it that they were shaped exactly alike and that each was as good as the other. As he made them he thought how much quicker his fingers were now at moulding things than they had been when he first tried. By evening the owls were dried out, so he put them in his pouch and loped back across the moorland towards the shore. He thought he would put the lamp-black and hoof glue on them tomorrow, for he was not yet very good at making fires.

He was quite happy, running in the late sunlight, and he made up a little song to keep time to his running.

'Oak and ash and holly and thorn,
In spring the bleating lambs are born;
Thorn and holly and ash and oak,
In winter their wool will clothe the folk.'

It was not a very good song, he thought, but it was better than nothing for running to, and it seemed to help his stiff leg along. He had not tried to make songs before and now he wondered if he could get to be as good at songs as he was at making shapes. He dreamed himself standing up by the hearth fire in the blackness of winter when there was nothing to do, when folk were waiting for the sun to come again so that they could go out into the field and scratch the earth with pointed sticks and then scatter the grain into the furrows. He thought how much the folk might like to hear his songs then, under the rush lights and with the snow piled up outside the door. Songs would make the folk merry and would help to pass the dark time along.

He was still thinking these things when he came to the cliff edge and looked down in horror at the shore below. The houses were still smouldering, and old folk and women lay about among the rocks. Some of them sprawled with their heads in the sea, being pushed up and down as the water came in and went out again. There was blood on them.

He scrambled down the loose shale and ran from place to place. There was no one to answer him. The River folk had all gone. Those folk who were left would not speak again.

Then he knew why the young war-men had whispered to one another and he felt very angry with them. He felt angry with Wander and Adder as well. They must have ordered this to be done.

Then he stopped being angry and grew afraid in case Blackbird lay among those on the shore. He went from one to the other, but could not find her.

After a while he sat on a flat rock wondering what to do next. They had not left any round boats behind and the only way he knew to get to the village by the river was along the shore in a boat. He could not think how you would get there going on foot inland.

He wished he had not gone away to find clay for the owls. Then he got angry with the owls for causing this, and took them from his pouch and ground them back to dust under his foot. But when he had done this he felt very foolish because he had taken such trouble to shape them well, and might never make anything as good again. He felt as sad as when he had first put the spear-stick into Shark that day, only sad in another way. He did not like spoiling anything, whether he had made it or not.

He did not dare stay in the village that night, with all the old folk and women and children lying about in silence. So he went back up the cliff and found a tree to get into, away from wolves. He did not sleep much that night, because he kept thinking that he was the cause of what had happened down on the shore. If he had not left the village he could have stopped the war-men from doing it.

Sometimes as he sat in the fork of the tree his running song came back into his head; but it was not very pleasing now. It gave him no happiness at all. He wished he had not made it, because it sounded a bad song to be thinking of when you remembered all the stiff folk lying in the sea with their houses burned down.

Once in the darkness a beast stopped under the tree and began to sniff up at him. He tried to smell what beast it was, but the wind blew the wrong way and he could only guess that it was some sort of cat because it spent a long time howling and sharpening its claws. And when he heard this he became very afraid, because a beast with claws could climb up into the trees and drag men down. At first he thought he should go higher up the tree, to where the thin branches were and where a big beast could not walk. But he was too frightened to move, and before dawn the beast went away, howling and grunting and scratching at the turf in anger.

When it was clear daylight he came down the tree and set off towards some woods that looked a misty blue in the sunshine. He thought the river might lie beyond the woods and that he might find Blackbird there.

IT WAS a thick wood and he was only in the middle of it when the dusk came again. That day he ate only some red berries off a bush, but he found a stream where the water was clear and sweet, so he did not go thirsty. Sometimes in the village where he was born the war-men would go for three days without eating when they were on their way to another village for a raid. But they had to have water to drink, or they would have died, they said. When they got to be very hungry on a raid, they would chew the bark of a tree. And when they got very thirsty and there was no water they would suck a smooth round pebble.

Twilight thought of these things in the deep wood. He looked round for a tree to climb into, but they were all so straight and tall, and their lowest branches were too high for him to reach. He became very frightened then and wished he knew how to make fire so that the red flames would keep the beasts away in the night. He tried to strike sparks off the stones that lay about, but he only knocked the skin off his knuckles. He thought how clever women were, to know how to make fire even from the time when they were little girls, almost too young to talk. He broke a young holly tree down and tore off all the side shoots. Then he bit at the end of it to make a spear-stick. It was not a very good one and would not have hurt a hare, much less a strong wolf with a thick hide. But he thought that if a wolf came and saw it in his hand, the wolf might think it was sharper than it was, and go away.

Once, his father Thorn had taught him a few words of the wolf language and he tried to remember them now. Words like 'I am savage. Go away. There is nothing for you here.' But he could not string all these words together because his teeth were chattering so much. He knew that if he said them to a man wolf, the beast would know he was afraid and would laugh at him. He thought he had better just point the spear-stick at the wolf and shout out as harshly as he could, and perhaps stamp on the dry ground with his good foot.

But no wolf came. And at dawn he went on through the tangled wood, not feeling at all sure now that he was on the right track towards the river.

To pass the time through the tangled forest, Twilight began to think about how things were shaped, from stone or clay or metal. Then all at once a thought came to him that stopped him as he walked. It came so fiercely and clearly into his head that he could not breathe for a while. He had to lean on a tree to keep from falling down with excitement. Then he became very frightened to think that he should know what he had just been told from somewhere. He knew that sometimes among the tribes those who were to go into the fire to bring a good harvest had strange dreams and knew things that other men did not know. He had heard the women talk of this often, and he wondered if what he now knew meant that he was going into the harvest fire somewhere.

He sat down with his back to a broad oak so that nothing could get at him from behind, and went over his dream again. If he was doomed to be put in the fire, he wanted to be quite sure that he really knew the

dream. It would be a waste to go into the fire if one had forgotten the dream. That would be a bad bargain. So he said to himself: All things come by shaping. Without shape there is nothing. Men are shaped. To shape a brooch you can take clay between the fingers and let them form it while it is wet. Then the sun helps to dry it. But to make a stone brooch you scratch the figure first on the flat stone, then get a harder stone chisel and chip pieces away. The hard chisel helps to make the shape. Now, there is another way, the way I have just dreamed in my head.

He had to stop there because the dream was not running clearly in his head, like a brook, now. And also because a young hare had come out of some fern and was sitting listening to him with its head on one side. Twilight did not wish to eat the hare because among his folk the hare was not to be touched. Its flesh was forbidden meat. But he did not want the hare to know his dream either. So he whistled and looked up into the sky as though he was only thinking of clouds and birds. The hare got tired and went away. He heard its feet bearing down on the dry crackling bracken and smiled to himself, thinking that this beast could not carry away his dream to tell to the other hares, to spread it round.

Then when all was silent he began again. He said to himself: When I pour hoof glue over a clay shape, the glue takes the shape of the clay. It goes into even the little scratches and takes their form. Suppose I made a big scratch and poured glue into it? The glue would take that form too. Suppose I scratched out the shape of a wolf and poured glue into that shape, then when the glue had hardened and I picked it out gently with a flint point, I would have the wolf shaped in glue.

He grew so excited then that he stood up and began to hit the tree with a stick, just for something to do, because his dream was coming clearer than ever.

Then he grew quiet once more and sat down. Now, he said to himself, glue melts in fire, it melts in rain, it is not hard and it does not last. But suppose there is something that lasts? Something that would first of all melt and run into the shape, and then grow hard and last a man's lifetime? Clay will not do that, for clay goes back to dust when it is dry Stone will not do it, for stone will not melt. What is there that will melt and then go hard again?

Suddenly he remembered the red copper that Wander had given him to shape. He remembered how soft that was, under his flint knife. It was so exciting, he almost began to cry. But then he stopped being excited and grew angry at everything. How can a man melt this copper? he said. A clay cooking pot would fall into dust if a man put copper into it and tried to melt it.

He got up, feeling cheated, furious. He struck at the bushes about him and a little brown snake slithered out and ran away from him in terror, leaving its curly shape in the dust with each wriggle of its body.

And as he watched the snake, the deep part of the dream came into his head so hard that he did weep now and the water ran like a stream on to his bare chest. Yes, first take stone, for stone lasts for ever and does not fall to dust. Then, with a chisel of hard flint, hollow the stone into the form of a cooking pot. Put the copper in that. Build a great hot fire and set the pot on it. Let the copper melt. And then, and then. . . .

He was out of the forest now, and suddenly knew that he had gone the wrong way. Everything felt wrong. The smell of the place was wrong too. It had a very old smell, as though men had been there for many lifetimes. Not like the place by the river where all smelled clean and still new, washed by the clear water.

And while he was still stumbling along and sniffing his way, he almost fell into a little hollow where there was a hearth fire smoking. A handful of men sat about it, and as they turned and gazed up at him, he was more frightened than if he had fallen into a pit of snakes.

THE MEN were so alike that they looked like one man many times over. Twilight saw their flat heads and slow yellow-grey eyes; the broadness of their noses and their wide mouths. They had dark lips and the teeth that showed between them were ground down and the colour of whalebone. Most of all that frightened him was the reddish hair that grew on their arms and chests and shoulders. In his head he named them the Red Men. He saw their big stomachs and short legs and thick arms. He had never seen such arms, or such hands. The palms were long but the fingers short. The nails on the fingers looked as black as their lips. They gazed at him slowly and scratched with these finger-nails at their shaggy reddish cheeks, or pulled at their loose lips.

At first he thought they would leap up and come for him. But they did not move, and when he glanced round the hollow he saw that they had no spears or bows with them. One of them was holding a flat stone and throwing it up a little way then catching it, but that was the only weapon Twilight could see.

He nodded down at them and smiled. One of the Red Men bared his teeth still further, as though it was in a snarl. But they did not nod, or wave when he waved. They only gazed at him silently.

It was all so for the space of many breaths. Then they all looked away from him, as though they had lost interest, and held their round bodies towards the fire to get as much heat from it as they could before it died down to white ash.

Twilight thought of turning away, back into the forest; but then he thought that if he did, they might rush after him and take him. So he did the other thing and holding his hands out before him so that they should see he carried no weapons, he went down into the hollow.

The scent that lay there was so heavy and raw, he had to hold his breath for a time. Then he got used to it and almost forgot it. And when he stood near them, the biggest of them moved slowly sideways to give him room to get near the fire. He went forward slowly, and one with smaller arms than the others reached out and touched him with short furry fingers. Twilight let himself be touched, though he almost shrank from the black nails. Yet the touch was as gentle as when a moth comes down on to a man's back.

Then the smaller Red Man made a rumbling sound in his chest and the others leaned forward and touched Twilight, feeling his smooth brown skin, squeezing his arm muscles gently, even pulling at his long shiny black hair. It was all done so lightly and gently. Twilight could not believe they could be so gentle.

And each time they did this they rumbled and their whole bodies seemed to nod to one another, as though they could speak without words.

At last Twilight plucked up his courage and said in Dog talk, 'I am looking for Blackbird. Have you seen her? She is very pretty and has leaves and flowers tattooed on her. There is no one like her.'

The Red Men looked down at the ground, then at each other, then scratched their hairy cheeks. They did not seem to hear him.

Twilight said very slowly, 'Where is your village?'

The one with the flat stone suddenly dropped it on to the ground as though it meant nothing to him any longer. The biggest of the Red Men swayed back and forth on his rock and then picked up a stick and scratched at the fire ash, scattering it about the hollow.

All at once they rose and shambled up the slope to the top, and Twilight thought that they would leave him by their white ashes. But the big one stopped and looked down at him, without speaking or moving his hands, and Twilight knew that they were waiting for him to go with them. He did not dare refuse.

He went last, far behind them, hardly able to keep up with their thick, short legs. He stood two heads taller than any of them, but he saw that they were twice as heavy as he was. One of them could have picked him up like a corn doll and have flung him ten paces away. He thought he knew now why they carried no weapons. Such men would not need to defend themselves very often.

Once as they crossed the moorland, an old dog wolf got up from under a bush where he had been sleeping and stood in their way, snarling, his hair bristling. But they went on and the wolf dropped his tail between his legs and scuttled away into the dark bushes.

They went in single file, the big one leading and the

small one at the end. Twilight knew that it would be useless to try to break away from them. They could have caught him without trouble, and have destroyed him with one twist of their powerful long hands.

At last, by dusk, they came to a rocky outcrop where no trees grew. And there he saw many cave holes. The setting sun made the rock red in colour. It was the same colour as the men. He knew that this was their home. It was far away from any other men.

THEY WENT through many tunnels, until at last they stood in a great round cavern where Twilight could stand upright. In the middle of the rock floor burned a great fire set round with stones. Piles of dried grass and brown fern lay against the walls.

At the far end waited a crowd of smaller Red Folk, some of them with less hair and with sharper teeth. One of these came up to Twilight and stroked his smooth face. He thought that this one even smiled at him, so he stroked this one's face, trying not to pull away from the shaggy mask. Then all at once he knew that this must be one of their young women, for she held her face close to him again to be stroked. The men who had brought him stood nodding with their thick bodies and rumbling in their chests.

Twilight felt very hungry. He turned gently and went to the big one and pointed to his open mouth. Big One gazed at him with flat amber-grey eyes for a time, then put out his hands and felt inside Twilight's mouth to touch his teeth. Twilight let this happen, then shook his head and made the movement of chewing tough meat. Big One suddenly turned away and rumbled at one of the smaller folk. She came running with a square of hide on which lay nuts and wild apples. Twilight smiled and nodded and took them. They were not the best food he had eaten, but they were welcome then. And when he had eaten these, the woman came again with a white cheese in her hands. She was squeezing it as she came, making the whey run out. Twilight did not care for such food, but he took it and ate it. Then Big One rumbled again and the woman fetched water in her cupped hands. And when Twilight had lapped at it, she wiped the rest of it on his hair and face, and snarled. He knew then that this was their smile. It was not meant to be savage.

He sat down near the fire. Big One rumbled in his chest and all the Red Folk came and stood round Twilight. He smiled and nodded at them all, but they did not smile or nod in return. He spoke to them in all the tongues he knew, but they did not answer.

Some of them were getting tired of him, he could tell. They were turning away and snatching up pieces of fern and breaking them. They were restless in their movements and were making short grunting sounds and bouncing a little on the soles of their hairy feet.

Twilight bent down and picked up a dropped twig. With it, in the grey dust by the hearth fire, he swiftly drew a leaping wolf.

They watched him in silence, then suddenly began to prance and beat their chests. Big One leaned forward and took Twilight by the ear and drew him to his side. All at once they began to snarl-laugh and touch Twilight. It was like an army of moths lighting on him. Then Big One held him so close that Twilight almost stifled in the thick reddish hair. But still he smiled. Then the woman put another twig in his hand and pointed to a spot by one of the fern beds. Twilight drew away from Big One and sketched a flying eagle with five strokes.

Then the cavern was alive with rumbling and dancing. And Big One came to Twilight and took his ear in those big teeth and nibbled it gently as though he was pleased with the eagle. Then all the young men lifted Twilight on to their shoulders and carried him along the winding tunnels, sometimes forgetting that the roofs were low and they held him high in honour. His head was bumped and his back scraped by the rock, but he laughed now, ignoring such small things.

And at last they came into the inmost cave which rose in the centre like a dome and echoed with the sounds of shuffling feet and chest rumbling and snarl laughter. And here, by the light of thin reed-flares, Twilight saw something he had never even dreamt of —a whole cavern covered with coloured shapes. The

Red Folk stood in silence watching him. He saw all the beasts of the land—bulls and wolves, foxes, dogs and wild cat. He saw eagles and owls, hawks and gulls, and a hundred small birds he had never even set eyes on before.

They were drawn round in black, and tinted in with yellow and red, green and white. Here and there he saw blue that signified the summer sky, and circles of reddish-gold that meant the sun.

And every lump and bump of the rock walls had been used, sometimes to mean the bulging back of the wild bulls, sometimes the curve of the eagle's breast.

And among all these creatures on the walls ran men with spears and bows, thin, black shaped men, hunting the creatures, fetching them down with skill and craft.

Twilight shook his head with bewilderment. Tears ran from his eyes down his cheeks. To be among such

makers, he thought! To live with men who did not need to kill other men, who were too strong even for the fierce wolf to attack! Who did not even need to talk!

He turned to Big One and held out his hand. Big One placed a charcoal stick in it and then watched. Twilight reached up and felt the smooth pale rock until he found a long bump in the surface, then with swift strokes he made a running stag, its antlers flaring out, the dust rising from beneath its hard hooves.

Big One took hold of his reddish cheek hair and began to tug at it, stamping his feet up and down. The other men did the same, until the domed cavern vibrated with the sound.

Then he went to Twilight and picked him up like a child and swung him into the air, passing him to the next man, and so to the next. And each of the Red Men slapped him on the back or nibbled at his ears, or tugged his hair—but always so gently that it was as though they thought he might break in their strong hands.

Then, when they had set him down, the men and women took charcoal sticks and drew on the walls, each in his own place, stags and stags and stags—as though Twilight had given them a new magic to make.

And at last they were all so weary and so happy that they went back to the fire-cave and lay on the fern beds, snarl-laughing at one another and gazing at Twilight with bright golden eyes.

Then the young woman who had brought the food to Twilight came and sat beside him and stroked his black hair with her furry hand. He was about to stroke her shaggy head when something told him not to. He saw that she wore about her thick neck a hide thong on which hung a shining black stone. And now he remembered that Big One also wore such a stone. So he did not stroke the woman, but looked away from her and snarl-laughed with the men. And after a while the woman got up and went to the dark part of the cave, among the other women and the furry children.

And in the morning, much before dawn, Big One came to Twilight and stood before him, looking into his eyes so softly that Twilight thought the chief was sad, and he wished that he could speak the Red Folk's language. Then all at once Twilight knew in his head that Big One was saying: 'What do you want? What can we do for you?'

Twilight took up the charcoal stick and drew Blackbird in the dust of the floor. At first he was afraid that he could not make the right shape, to show how her face was different from other faces; but his hand caught his dream and he drew her so rightly that he felt she might speak to him from the dust. He even drew her pretty tattoo-markings.

Big One stared down at Blackbird's shape for a long space, then nodded with all his body. But his eyes carried something else in them, as though he was not sure. So Twilight made two other shapes—one of Wander and the other of Adder the war-man carrying his spear. And when he had drawn these two he shook his head and waved his open hand from side to side, to tell Big One that these were not folk he wanted to make him happy.

Big One snarl-laughed then and seemed to understand. Then he turned and rumbled in his chest at the young men. They gathered round and gazed down at the floor-shapes and nodded with their bodies. But one of them, with brighter eyes than the others, and light yellowish hair on his body, suddenly touched Twilight on the chest and then swayed his head sideways with his eyes wide open and puzzled, as though to ask where Blackbird could be found. Twilight bent again and drew the river, with the hills behind it and the huts along the bank among the reeds. Then he put boats on the river with men fishing in them, and the long shelter where the folk gathered to be fed by Wander.

Yellow One nodded with his body then stubbed his his thick forefinger right in the middle of the river as though he knew where this place could be found.

The Red Men began their dance, beating on their chests and grunting through their broad noses. And when they had finished this, Big One's daughter who wore the black stone brought them nuts and white roots on broad green leaves, and after they had eaten, they bent low and ran from the cavern.

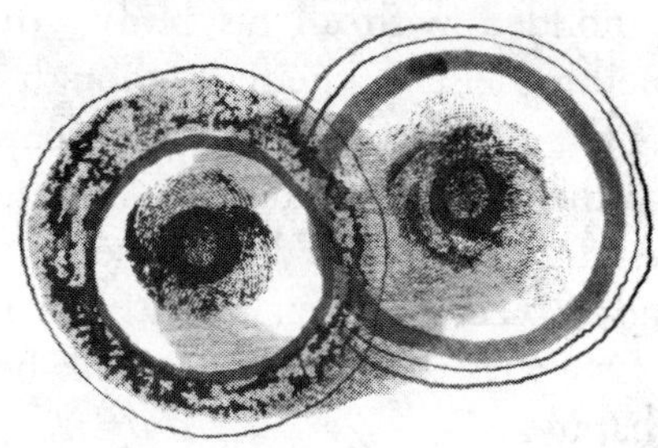

TWILIGHT was afraid they would never come back. He sat outside the cavern and watched the moon come and go, round the sky. It was quite safe to be out there, because no wolves ever dared prowl near that place.

When the sun came up again, Twilight thought that it had all been a dream. The old ones and women did not come near him, but stayed in the farthest cavern, with their babies and children.

Only Big One's daughter came to him and gave him white roots and nuts and cheese to eat. Later she gave him meat of some sort, but she held it away from her as though she did not care to touch it and he did not like the smell of it, so flung it into a heather clump when she had gone away.

He tried to find his way back into the dream-cavern where all the coloured creatures were; but the old men crouched in the tunnel glaring at him all hairy and he did not dare try to pass them. It was a forbidden place when Big One was not there to give permission.

Then at dusk the Red Men came back. They were carrying Blackbird on a litter made of woven boughs. She was very frightened till she saw Twilight, then she ran to him and put her arms round him and laughed into his face. The Red Men watched this, then began their grunting dance, beating their chests and making the dust fill the cave.

And when the dance was over and Blackbird had stopped hugging Twilight, Yellow One came to them and flung a bundle at their feet like an offering. In the dusk, Twilight could not tell what it was, but when he got a rushlight and bent over it, he saw that Wander and Adder must have lost most of their hair.

He snarl-laughed at Yellow One, as though he was pleased; but as soon as he could, he took the bundle and dropped it down into a hole in the ground forty paces away from the caverns.

Blackbird saw this and said, 'If they had beaten you as they beat me, you would not look so sad. See, there are marks on me that I shall never lose.'

Twilight said, 'That is a small thing. To lose one's hair is a big thing. Wander had great pride in her hair. It was the colour of corn in the sunlight.'

Blackbird laughed at him and said, 'The biggest thing for us is to be together again and to be happy. But I do not think that Big One's daughter is happy; she looks at me as though she wishes to bite me.'

Twilight said, 'She will come to like you if you are

kind to her and do not sniff at the food she finds for us. Perhaps one day she will let you go out and help to find the food too.'

Blackbird said, 'Yes, and I will teach her to spin wool and to weave. We shall be like sisters together.'

Twilight said, 'It will be better when we have learned how to speak with them. I have tried, but it hurts my chest to make the words they make. I can only speak to them with my shapes. We are so different, but our shapes bring us together like brothers and sisters. I thought that I was the only man who could make shapes, but each one of the Red folk, even the youngest, can make much better shapes than I can. But when I have found out the way to make my things in copper, melted in the fire, then they will see something!'

Blackbird screwed up her nose. 'Shapes in melted copper?' she said. 'I think you are dreaming again. You are the strangest man I have met. That is why I like you.'

Twilight said, 'I like you just because you are Blackbird. I do not have to have things to like folk for. I like them just because they are themselves. You are my sister and we can talk and laugh together when we say strange things. To be able to laugh, that is a big thing. Without laughter life is very black.'

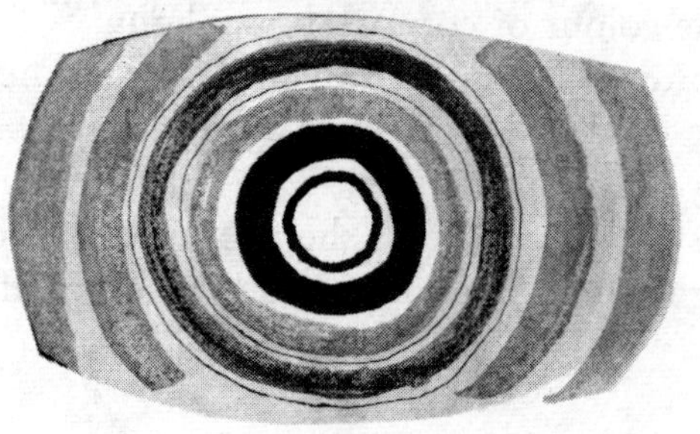

SO THEY stayed with the Red Folk. Big One gave them a little cave to be in when they felt like talking and laughing together. Yellow One sometimes took Twilight into the domed cavern and showed him how to put the colours on to the wall, to make all the wild creatures look more real. Once Yellow One covered Twilight's hand with red clay-paint and then pressed it on to the wall so as to leave its shape there for ever. Then he put paint on his own hand and placed it beside Twilight's on the wall so that they were together, like the hands of two close friends. Big One came in when this was being done, and put his great arms round both of them, hugging them. He was so strong that Twilight felt the breath go out of his body and he hoped that Big One would not squeeze any harder in case his bones broke.

At this time, Blackbird taught Big One's daughter how to spin and weave. The Red Men went out every day to find scraps of wool left on bushes, and brought them back proudly as though they had done something very important. Blackbird made herself a little loom over which she criss-crossed the strands of wool when she had rolled them between her hands into a rough yarn. This loom could only make small squares of loosely woven cloth, but Blackbird stitched the pieces together and at last made a skirt for Big One's daughter. As the Red Men sat round, watching the cloth growing in size each day, they grunted and beat their chests and bobbed up and down, as though this was the most wonderful thing they had ever seen. Big One's daughter let Blackbird put the skirt on her, but after a while took it off again and placed it on a shelf in the cave where it would be safe. She tried very hard to make cloth like Blackbird, but her fingers were so strong that she always broke the wool. At last she grew so impatient that she broke the loom into pieces and threw it away. Then she was sorry for what she had done, and went out every day, even when the weather got to be much colder, to fetch good things for Blackbird to eat. Once Blackbird tried to make porridge for the Red Folk, from acorns which she had dried and roasted, but they spluttered and spat this porridge out.

Then a bad thing happened quite suddenly. One day Big One's daughter did not come back from the woods when she went to gather roots. The Red Folk in the cave waited until it was almost dusk, then they began to stare at one another and to sniff and bob up and down. They made little restless movements with their fingers and tore at pieces of fern. Sometimes the reddish hair on their backs seemed to stand up straight and they made low growling sounds in their stomachs.

Big One went to the cave entrance many times and stared out towards the woods, sniffing and grunting to himself. Yellow One joined him and did the same. Their yellowish eyes were wide and gleaming. They kept plucking at the hair on their faces.

At last, when they could stand it no longer, the two of them ran off towards the trees and were away until the moon rose high above the caves. And when they came back, Big One was carrying his daughter. There were four arrows in her chest, two of them broken off short as though she had tried to snatch them out.

Twilight looked at the arrows and said to Blackbird, 'I have seen arrows like these before,' he said, 'and so have you.'

She nodded. 'They are the work of the River Folk,' she said. 'And this one, with the black feathers on it, belongs to Adder. He sent this one into her.'

While they were talking, Big One watched them carefully, his eyes and nostrils wide, as though he was trying to sniff in all the words they spoke to understand them.

Twilight turned to him and made the motion of shooting an arrow, then took a strand of his own hair and stretched it out. Big One seemed to know then that it had been Wander and Adder who had ambushed his daughter.

That night, Twilight heard the Red Men going off into the woods. He saw their shadows passing the mouth of the little cave where he lay, and knew that this time they were taking spear-sticks with them.

He said, 'All this is because of me. If I had stayed with the River Folk, Big One's daughter would not be dead. They have tracked you here and this is their revenge.'

Blackbird said, 'You did not do it, brother. It must be Wander. She is a bad woman who wants everything for herself. She has told Adder to do it. You did not do it. Do not weep.'

But Twilight shook his dark head and said, 'It is because of my pictures. They were the beginning of all the bad things in my life. If I had not drawn that wolf in the longhouse, perhaps my mother would still be alive. And perhaps little Bud would not have died either.'

Blackbird could tell that it was useless to talk to him at this time, he was so deep in his dreams of all the things that had happened.

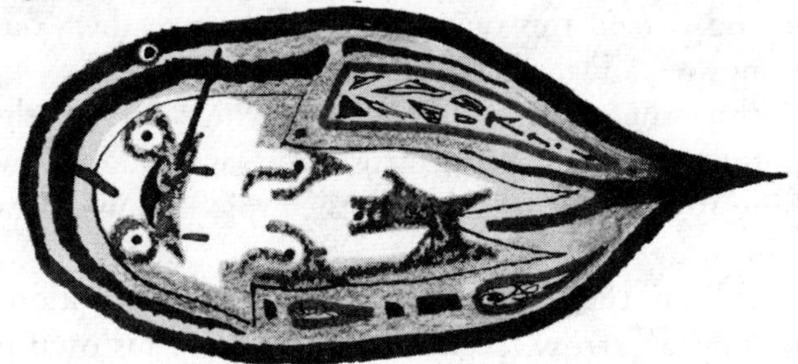

IN THE morning the Red Men came back to the caves. Some of them had been hurt with arrows, and Big One had a cut across his cheek from an axe. But they seemed pleased with what they had done. Yellow One came to Twilight and quickly sketched the shape of the village by the river, then drew his hand across it as though to wipe it out.

Then he called to one of the other Red Men who came shambling up with something wrapped in a woollen shawl. He gave it to Blackbird who was afraid to open it at first, but then it began to move in her hands, and she pulled back the wrappings and said, 'Look, it is a baby.'

Twilight looked down at it for a while and then said, 'See, it is wearing the copper thing I made, round its neck. This must be Wander's baby. But how will it live, with no mother to care for it any longer?'

Blackbird said, 'We have no quarrel with a little

baby, brother. This little thing has hurt no one and killed no one. We can look after it, and when it grows you can show it how to draw shapes and make things.'

This was in the bad time of the year, when the snow stayed so long that great stags came out of the woods and nibbled at the rotten black thatch of the storehouses.

They called the baby Linnet because her hair had the glints of many colours in it, and Twilight remembered that he had once seen a linnet with seven different colours in its feathers. At first Linnet's temper was not as pretty as she was. If she grew angry she yelled till her face went a deep red like the colour of sandstone. And she flailed her little arms and legs till the wicker basket that Twilight had made for her fell to shreds. Worst of all, she kept screeching when Twilight wanted to make his pictures.

He said, 'I can face many things. You know how I once stood against Shark of the Fish Folk with his fearful axe. But I cannot put up with Linnet's howling. It drives all the pictures out of my head. She should know better than to howl all the time and to kick her basket to pieces. This upsets a picture man.'

Blackbird smiled and said, 'You men are so stupid. It is only for a little time, then Linnet will wear a coloured skirt and a necklace of blue beads, and then all the fierce young men with black beards will come rushing to ask for her, shaking their axes.'

Twilight went to think about this in his own dark corner, where he drew his most important things. He said at last, 'When I have a dog, I know that the dog is mine. It will come when I call its name. The dog is

for me and no black bearded young men come asking for it. Linnet is mine and no one shall take her away.'

Blackbird said softly, 'We are not talking about dogs. We are talking about menfolk, who are the masters of dogs. We are talking about folk who go like trees, upright, and can make pictures on earth or on clay. Now, dogs cannot do that. They cannot throw spears. They are not the same.'

Twilight gazed into the fire for a long space; then he said, 'I know that dogs cannot throw spears. Only a woman would say a foolish thing like that. But I will remind you that dogs can bite. They have fangs, but men have no fangs. Dogs do not need spears, you see, my foolish sister.'

In the end Blackbird had to give in. Of course dogs had fangs and men had no fangs. It didn't seem worth arguing about. She could not understand how menfolk came to speak the words they did, and with such serious faces too. Besides, Linnet was so pretty that it was a waste of such a baby not to keep looking at her all the time. That was better than silly quarrelling.

Big One and the Red Folk thought she was pretty too. They stood near Twilight's cave door watching her and would not go away. When Blackbird let them handle her they did it as though she were a bird's egg that would break. Blackbird laughed at them and said, 'She is as strong as a little wolf. See, you can throw her up into the air.'

But Big One would not let the folk do that. He even snarled when Blackbird did it to show them. And when Linnet was older, Big One was happiest for the child to crawl about in his great cavern. He taught her the picture-making and let her ride on his back.

Linnet learned to speak the Red Folk language before she spoke her own. This made Twilight angry, just as the women's language had made him angry when he was a boy. 'She will be growing red hair all over her back next,' he said. But he stopped sulking in his dark corner when Linnet took a stick and drew on the earth floor. She drew creatures she had never seen, and made them so swiftly, with so few strokes, that Twilight loved her more than his right hand. He said, 'No black beard with an axe is going to have you, Linnet. Only the greatest of cave painters is worthy of you, my pretty.'

Blackbird came in and rubbed out the pictures with her bare foot. 'Come, Linnet,' she said, 'it is time for you to learn how to rub the sheep's wool between your hands to make thread. That is a woman's work, not this picture-dreaming. You shall learn to weave.'

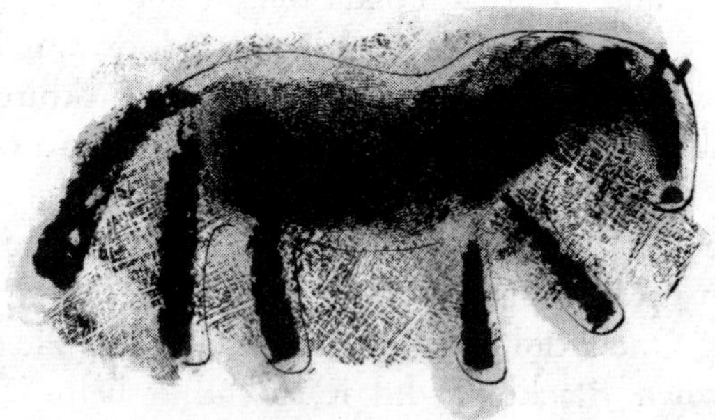

THEN THERE were three bad years, one following the other. Twilight could not get anything to grow in his little square field. Blackbird could not find nuts or berries or birds' eggs in the wood. The old folk of the Red Men lay down and died, or walked off into the forest and did not come back. No babies were born in the great cavern. It became very quiet and brooding in the darkness there.

Linnet grew so thin that Blackbird wept. Twilight drew all the flesh creatures he could think of, even hares, with arrows in them; but the hunting was poor all the same.

Then the worst of things happened. Big One came into Twilight's house and looked down at Linnet. He bent and felt how thin her arms were now, and his eyes were sad and sunken in his great shaggy head.

He tried to say words to Twilight but could not form them. At last he took a heavy spear-stick and walked into the forest alone. The snow had made the wolves brave. Seven of them waited for Big One, remembering how he had treated them in the past, and they rushed at him from all sides. They did not find it easy, even so, and four of them did not go back to their lairs. But the others dragged him down and then snarled at one another over him till nightfall.

After this Yellow One became the cavern chieftain.

One day he came to Twilight's house and stood there, holding out his hands for Linnet, as though he wished to take her away, but Blackbird shook her head. Then Yellow One went off sadly and the next morning there was a great stillness in the Red Folk's cavern. Twilight went to find out about it, and saw that the folk had all gone. They had left nothing behind them. They had even scratched away the coloured pictures from the walls.

Ash and bracken lay scattered all over the floors, and broken arrows and chewed bones. It was now like a forgotten midden.

TWILIGHT followed their tracks for a while into the deep forest. Then he came to a place where the snow was trampled and red, and the tracks seemed to go off in all directions. Dead wolves lay here and there, one of them even hanging across the bough of an oak tree limply, as though he had been flung there in fury. Among the spikes of the hawthorn and gorse, Twilight found scraps of reddish hair. Broken and stained spear-sticks lay all about.

He was afraid then to go farther into the forest, and turned and ran back as fast as he could to the little cave. When he had told Blackbird what he had seen, she said, 'I think that the Red Folk are finished now. We have seen the last of them. They were the first of the folk in the land and now they have gone to quiet places to die. There will be no more pictures in the caves. We were the only folk to see them. Now no one will ever know about them.'

Twilight could not bear to think of this. He said, 'Such pictures should last for ever. Why should a man be born to put his dreams on the walls if they are to be wiped away and never be seen again? If you make a little piece of cloth, you take care of it and do not waste it. Yet pictures, which are from the deepest inside of a man's heart, are wasted because of folk like Wander and Adder, and because of brutish creatures like the forest wolves. Why is this? Tell me, Blackbird, why is this?'

Blackbird said, 'I cannot tell you, brother. I am not a dreamer like you and like the Red Folk. I am a woman. All I can tell you is that the wolves will come closer and closer to our cave now that the Red Folk are gone. We cannot deal with wolves, and we have Linnet to think of.'

Twilight said, 'What should we do, to save little Linnet, then?'

Blackbird said, 'She is very thin and white. She has not laughed or spoken for many days. She has not opened her eyes today at all. If we do not think of something she will go from us into a long sleep and not come back.'

Twilight got up and went into his dark corner where the dreams came to him usually. And after a while he went back to Blackbird and said, 'Dreams are well enough. Pictures are well enough. But there is something stronger than dreams and pictures. I have just smelled it.'

Blackbird said, 'What is it, brother? Tell me what you have smelled.'

He said, 'I cannot describe it, Blackbird. It is not a thing, it is inside the head and has no shape. It is like a strength, but it is not in the arms or legs or body. It cannot hold a spear-stick or an axe, but it is above those things. It is a sort of fierceness that is more than hurting someone, it is something so strong that if a wolf sniffed it he would turn and go away.'

Blackbird said gently, 'Are you quite sure of this, brother?'

Twilight nodded. 'Yes, yes,' he said. 'I can feel it now, inside my head. It makes me not afraid of wolves or anything. It will protect little Linnet, I am sure of that.'

So Blackbird said quietly, 'Very well, while this is in you, let us go away from here and find another place where there are folk we can speak to, folk who have sheep milk and bread and meat for the little one.'

They wrapped her in a sheepskin bundle, and a woollen shawl, and then set off away from the forest, towards the open land that lay beyond the nearest ridge of hills.

And when they had gone for a while a clan of brown wolves started up from behind a little clump of hawthorn trees and came snuffling towards them. Blackbird gave a little scream, but Twilight turned on her with such a stern face that she even smiled at him.

He said, 'Hold tight to Linnet and I will speak to these poor four-footed things.'

But he did not have the chance to speak. He went forward at the clan-leader, who was already bristling to leap, and never said a word. The wolf halted suddenly and glared at him, his eyes flat and amber, his red tongue lolling out between the white fangs. But it did not leap. Instead, its hackles fell all at once and its tail dropped into the snow. It looked up at Twilight

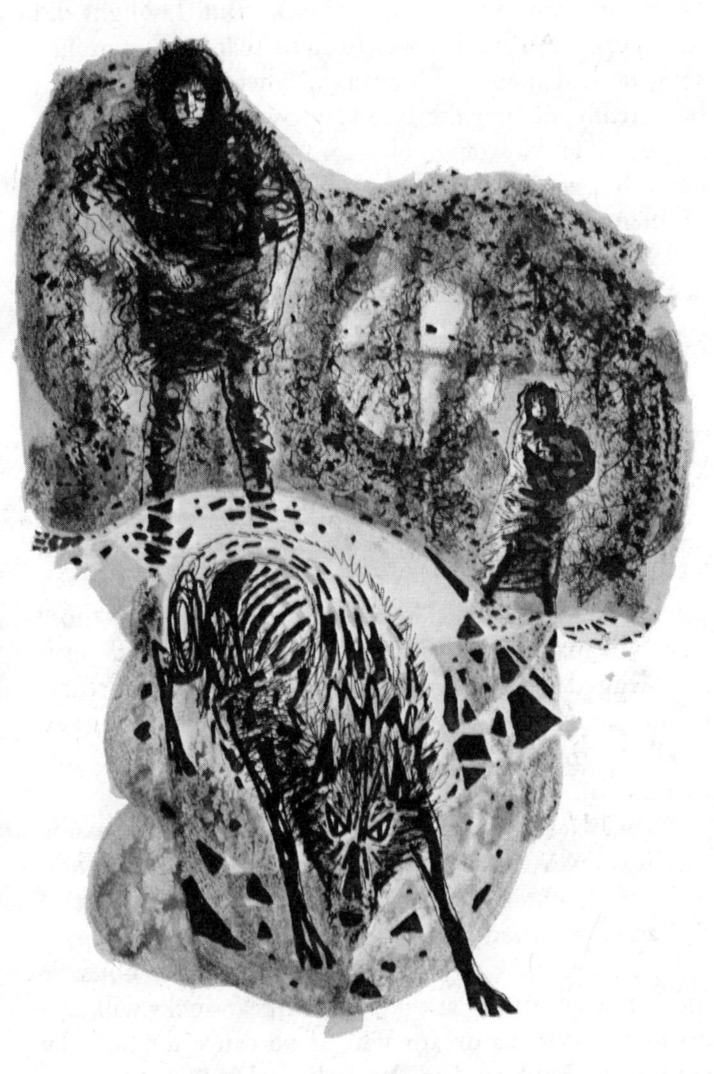

as though waiting for a command. But Twilight did not speak. All he did was to hum that little running-song he had made, so long ago, when he was coming back from making the two clay owls. The king wolf heard this and a strange blur came across his flat yellow eyes. It was almost as though his hair came down over his brows in a bewildered frown. Then, when Twilight still kept coming on, the wolf turned his head slowly, not to look at him, and then slunk round and went back to his folk.

Blackbird came running up and laughing. She said, 'See, they have drawn back into the bushes. They cannot face you, brother. What did you say to their king?'

Twilight looked at her vacantly, the beads of sweat on his lips and chin. 'Say to them?' he said. 'It would be a very small man who bothered to argue with such carrion-folk. It would be a waste of manhood if those who can make pictures should have to deal with such four-legged scum as wolves. They smelled the pictures in me and drew away from them. Perhaps they smelled the other thing I once dreamed, of forming an owl in melted copper.'

Then Blackbird said, smiling, 'If you talk such magic I shall draw away from you too, brother. For that is far more frightening than a spear-stick.'

Twilight turned towards her and said, 'I shall never carry a spear-stick any more. Spear-sticks did not save the Red Men, strong as they were. Spear-sticks will save no man. But his dream will, if he can only find the courage to hold it when the wolves glare into his eyes.'

Blackbird said, 'Hush! Hush! You are getting loud and boastful. You will waken the little sleeping Linnet in her sheepskin nest with your shouting.'

Twilight laughed and said, 'Let her wake, if she wishes. Let her see that I do not drag my leg now, that I have learned to walk as firmly as any man should do.'

Blackbird said, 'But if she wakes she will not be bothered about your silly leg, Twilight. She will be more concerned with feeling hungry. She will cry out because she has had no food for so many days. That is what Linnet will do.'

Twilight strode on for a while, then he said, 'For once I shall not go into a dark corner and tear out my hair because a child cries and disturbs my dreams. For now the child is a part of my dreams, and my dreams are for that child. She can cry to her heart's content, and soon she will cry no more, because there will be food and milk enough to make her smile again.'

Blackbird was a few paces behind, carrying the sleeping bundle gently so as not to set it squealing. She said, her head down and set towards the thick snow, 'Dreams, dreams, dreams! Men, men, men! I have heard it all before, whether they hold a charcoal stick or a spear.'

Then Twilight said very calmly, 'You are so locked in your own dreams of what you once saw that you do not see what lies before you, sister. Lift up your head and see something more than snow.'

So Blackbird looked up and saw the little village before them, warm among the gentle hills, with the blue smoke rising from the huts.

She said amazed, 'Look, brother, there is no stockade round this place.'

Twilight said, 'Stockade? Stockade? Must a man have a stockade? Is he born with a stockade about him? Is there a stockade round little Linnet now? I tell you, before I even see them, that the folk of this place have something better than stockades, or spear-sticks, to keep them safe. Come on, Blackbird, I can see that they are coming to meet us, laughing—as well they might, seeing our strange cavern-clothes!'

Then he went with his hand outstretched to meet them laughing too. And behind him Blackbird was laughing. And in her sheepskin bundle, Linnet had awakened and was doing her best to laugh.

It was a golden end to a black beginning indeed.

Postscript by

ROSEMARY SUTCLIFF

Different kinds of stories need to be told in different kinds of words strung together in different ways.

Henry Treece understood this better than almost any other writer I know. He had a very special gift for finding exactly the words and word-patterns that each of his books needed, so that instead of simply telling the story, they blend into it and become part of its texture and colour and shape and smell.

This is a kind of magic; but it is a magic that, if it is perfectly carried out, hardly shows; so that one might read *The Dream-time* from beginning to end, and never notice that it was there at all, which would be a great pity.

The Dream-time is a story of people in the very early morning of humanity, when they were not really used to being people at all, and so everything had a strangeness about it, and nothing was quite certain; not even that the spring would come again next year. They were so near the beginning that they can have had only the fewest and simplest of words with which to talk to each other and share their thoughts and feelings and ideas. And yet we know, from the things to do with their religion and way of life that they left behind them, and from Stone Age people who are alive today, such as the Bushmen of the Kalahari, that they had all kinds of complicated thoughts and fears and longings in their heads and hearts. So Henry Treece has told this story in very short and simple words, put together in such a way that they can express things which are not simple at all.

Before you have read very far into *The Dream-time*, you will know what Henry Treece is saying. Indeed, he makes Crookleg, who became Twilight, think part of it for him: 'He wished that all people, the men and women and horses and owls and dogs could agree to speak the same words. Then all things would be easy, to speak and to be understood. Perhaps no one would fight then.'

It is a constantly shifting and changing story that holds one all the way, with its adventures and its strange peoples and places; but it is also a plea for people to get to know each other and care about each other more; for peace instead of war, making instead of breaking.

I think that in this, the last book that Henry Treece wrote, he did not mean to make a historical novel, such as he had made before, but to do something quite different. It is more as though, in a way, he were writing down a dream; and just as, in a dream, times and places get jumbled together, he has deliberately put different periods and 'pockets' of very different Peoples nearer to each other than they really were. The story, of a boy who would rather make beautiful things than kill people, seems to belong to the late Stone Age, to the Little Dark People who possessed the secret of growing barley; but the Hunters, the makers of wonderful cave paintings, who were there long before the Barley People, come into it, too; and about the River Folk there is a suggestion of the Age of Bronze, which came after the Little Dark Ones had had their day. I think that in all this, he was trying to show that however much people change in the outward way that they behave and even think, certain things never change. Some of these things are good, and some of them bad and sad. In all ages, even today, there are people who want to make beautiful things more than anything else in the world; and people who are willing to die for a dream, even for the kind of dream that seems crazy to everyone else. And in all ages, even today when we have had four thousand years or so in which to learn more sense, people still fight because they do not understand each other.

One of the sad things of life, for every writer, is the knowing that one day he will write his last book. And all too often, when it comes, it is just a book like others that he has written before; maybe not even as good as some of those others were. But Henry Treece was lucky; he has written a very special book indeed for his last novel of all.

TITLES IN THE NEW WINDMILL SERIES

Chinua Achebe: *Things Fall Apart*
Louisa M. Alcott: *Little Women*
Elizabeth Allen: *Deitz and Denny*
Eric Allen: *The Latchkey Children*
Margery Allingham: *The Tiger in the Smoke*
Michael Anthony: *The Year in San Fernando*
Bernard Ashley: *A Kind of Wild Justice*
Enid Bagnold: *National Velvet*
Martin Ballard: *Dockie*
Stan Barstow: *Joby*
H. Mortimer Batten: *The Singing Forest*
Nina Bawden: *On the Run; The Witch's Daughter; A Handful of Thieves; Carrie's War; Rebel on a Rock; The Robbers*
Rex Benedict: *Last Stand at Goodbye Gulch*
Phyllis Bentley: *The Adventures of Tom Leigh*
Paul Berna: *Flood Warning*
Judy Blume: *It's Not the End of the World*
Pierre Boulle: *The Bridge on the River Kwai*
E. R. Braithwaite: *To Sir, With Love*
D. K. Broster: *The Gleam in the North*
F. Hodgson Burnett: *The Secret Garden*
Helen Bush: *Mary Anning's Treasures*
Betsy Byars: *The Midnight Fox*
A. Calder-Marshall: *The Man from Devil's Island*
John Caldwell: *Desperate Voyage*
Ian Cameron: *The Island at the Top of the World*
Albert Camus: *The Outsider*
Victor Canning: *The Runaways; Flight of the Grey Goose*
Charles Chaplin: *My Early Years*
Erskine Childers: *The Riddle of the Sands*
John Christopher: *The Guardians; The Lotus Caves; Empty World*
Richard Church: *The Cave; Over the Bridge; The White Doe*
Colette: *My Mother's House*
Alexander Cordell: *The Traitor Within*
Margaret Craven: *I Heard the Owl Call my Name*
Roald Dahl: *Danny, Champion of the World; The Wonderful Story of Henry Sugar; George's Marvellous Medicine*
Andrew Davies: *Conrad's War*
Meindert deJong: *The Wheel on the School*
Peter Dickinson: *The Gift; Annerton Pit*
Eleanor Doorly: *The Radium Woman; The Microbe Man; The Insect Man*
Gerald Durrell: *Three Singles to Adventure; The Drunken Forest; Encounters with Animals*
Elizabeth Enright: *The Saturdays*
J. M. Falkner: *Moonfleet*
C. S. Forester: *The General*
Jane Gardan: *The Hollow Land*
Eve Garnett: *The Family from One End Street; Further Adventures of the Family from One End Street*
G. M. Glaskin: *A Waltz through the Hills*
Rumer Godden: *Black Narcissus*
Kenneth Graham: *Wind in the Willows*
Graham Greene: *The Third Man* and *The Fallen Idol*
Grey Owl: *Sajo and her Beaver People*
John Griffin: *Skulker Wheat and Other Stories*
G. and W. Grossmith: *The Diary of a Nobody*
René Guillot: *Kpo the Leopard*
Jan De Hartog: *The Lost Sea*

TITLES IN THE NEW

Erik Haugaard: *The Little Fishes*
Esther Hautzig: *The Endless Steppe*
Bessie Head: *When Rain Clouds Gather*
Ernest Hemingway: *The Old Man and the Sea*
John Hersey: *A Single Pebble*
Nigel Hinton: *Getting Free; Buddy*
Alfred Hitchcock: *Sinister Spies*
C. Walter Hodges: *The Overland Launch*
Geoffrey Household: *Rogue Male; A Rough Shoot; Prisoner of the Indies; Escape into Daylight*
Fred Hoyle: *The Black Cloud*
Irene Hunt: *Across Five Aprils*
Henry James: *Washington Square*
Josephine Kamm: *Young Mother; Out of Step; Where Do We Go From Here?; The Starting Point*
Erich Kästner: *Emil and the Detectives; Lottie and Lisa*
M. E. Kerr: *Dinky Hocker Shoots Smack!; Gentlehands*
Clive King: *Me and My Million*
John Knowles: *A Separate Peace*
Marghanita Laski: *Little Boy Lost*
D. H. Lawrence: *Sea and Sardinia; The Fox* and *The Virgin and the Gypsy; Selected Tales*
Harper Lee: *To Kill a Mockingbird*
Laurie Lee: *As I Walked Out One Mid-Summer Morning*
Ursula Le Guin: *A Wizard of Earthsea; The Tombs of Atuan; The Farthest Shore; A Very Long Way from Anywhere Else*
Doris Lessing: *The Grass is Singing*
C. Day Lewis: *The Otterbury Incident*
Lorna Lewis: *Leonardo the Inventor*
Martin Lindsay: *The Epic of Captain Scott*
David Line: *Run for Your Life; Mike and Me; Under Plum Lake*
Kathleen Lines: *The House of the Nightmare; The Haunted and the Haunters*
Joan Lingard: *Across the Barricades; Into Exile; The Clearance; The File on Fräuline Berg*
Penelope Lively: *The Ghost of Thomas Kempe*
Jack London: *The Call of the Wild; White Fang*
Carson McCullers: *The Member of the Wedding*
Lee McGiffen: *On the Trail to Sacramento*
Wolf Mankowitz: *A Kid for Two Farthings*
Olivia Manning: *The Play Room*
Jan Mark: *Thunder and Lightnings; Under the Autumn Garden*
James Vance Marshall: *A River Ran Out of Eden; Walkabout; My Boy John that Went to Sea; A Walk to the Hills of the Dreamtime*
David Martin: *The Cabby's Daughter*
J. P. Martin: *Uncle*
John Masefield: *The Bird of Dawning; The Midnight Folk; The Box of Delights*
W. Somerset Maugham: *The Kite and Other Stories*
Guy de Maupassant: *Prisoners of War and Other Stories*
Laurence Meynell: *Builder and Dreamer*
Yvonne Mitchell: *Cathy Away*
Honoré Morrow: *The Splendid Journey*
Bill Naughton: *The Goalkeeper's Revenge; A Dog Called Nelson; My Pal Spadger*
E. Nesbit: *The Railway Children; The Story of the Treasure Seekers*
E. Neville: *It's Like this, Cat*
Mary Norton: *The Borrowers*
Wilfrid Noyce: *South Col*
Robert C. O'Brien: *Mrs Frisby and the Rats of NIMH; Z for Zachariah*
Scott O'Dell: *Island of the Blue Dolphins*
George Orwell: *Animal Farm*
Katherine Paterson: *Jacob Have I Loved*